Untold Story - 1946 Naval Mutiny

Last War of Independence

Untold Story - 1946 Naval Mutiny

Last War of Independence

by

Lt Cdr G D Sharma, VSM (Retd)

(Established 1870)

Centre For Armed Forces Historical Research
United Service Institution of India
New Delhi

Vij Books India Pvt Ltd

New Delhi (India)

Published by

Vij Books India Pvt Ltd
(Publishers, Distributors & Importers)
2/19, Ansari Road
Delhi – 110 002
Phones: 91-11-43596460, 91-11-47340674
Fax: 91-11-47340674
e-mail: vijbooks@rediffmail.com

Copyright © 2015, United Service Institution of India, New Delhi

ISBN (Pb)   : 9789385563003 (2016)

Contents

Author's Note

From time immemorial nations had waged wars to rule over others and expand their kingdom. India with its vast coast line & over 200 big & small ports flourished on sea trade but was not maritime Sea Force. Royal Navy ruled the seas and British subjugation of India is long history. The need to form Royal Indian Navy was British compulsion. After the war, in Feb 1946 Indian naval sailors revolted against British Naval authorities. It jolted British confidence and helped to revive and rekindle the national spirit against British injustice.

India achieved its independence on 15 August 1947 but it had hardly changed anything in the Navy. After Examination in Nov 1947 I joined HMIS 'Shivaji ' as naval Apprentice. It was the first batch of apprentices recruited after the Mutiny. It then had common basic workshop facilities & equipment required for Engine Room training only. Largely Royal Naval Officers were senior departmental & administrative officers. I was allotted 'Ordnance' branch. Hurriedly 'Ordnance Demonstration Room' was set up with obsolete & redundant naval guns for our training. I was a junior sailor and my pay scale was the same as paid to my pre-independence predecessors of the Navy. Ration scales were also same but rations were edibles & service conditions slightly better. The conduct of R N Officers projected their class superiority. Officers and Sailors were sent to R N establishments in U K for further training.

Navy was senior Service even after independence. It had also received 'President Colours' before other Services. Naval HQs was staffed by R N Officers. The navy carried British legacy. The newly independent Indian Navy was equipped with British war surplus & redundant naval ships and also naval branch structure required quick changes. The author also had undergone these professional changes in his career.

A number of books have been written on the 1946 naval mutiny but the true facts of this historic event remained untold. These were deliberately suppressed. The Inquiry Commission report gave graphic details of mutiny in all naval stations but it awarded no punishment to the guilty. It enumerated bad service conditions leading to mutiny but recommended no action against Naval Administration. The book attempts to bring out these and hitherto some unknown & deliberately hidden facts of 1946 Naval Mutiny.

After the war the atmosphere in India was politically surcharged and 1946 Naval Mutiny further vitalized it. Like the men of 1857 mutiny and Indian National Army the Indian Naval Sailors also openly defied British Authority. It "vas historic event. If the failure of 1857 mutiny & defeat of! NA had sadden Indian hearts the 1946 revolt by Indian Naval Sailors greatly helped & revived the spirit for Indian independence and freedom of India from British rule. It is noteworthy that all these uprisings were fought by men from all religions and coming from all parts of India. Naval mutiny was snuffed in shortest time but Indian Independence followed it and there were no further struggles for Independence of the country. Consequently the sailors who were discharged from service, though belated, were given due recognition of **FREEDOM FIGHTERS** by the Government of India. Indian Navy honored two leaders of this mutiny, Petty Officer Madan Singh & L Tel BC Dutt by naming two ocean going naval Tugs after their names. In 2001 the Indian Navy also laid a wreath and constructed R I N Memorial at Colaba, Bombay, the birth place of Naval Mutiny. During 1970-71, coinciding with silver jubilee year of 1946 Naval Mutiny, some leaflets/pamphlets were also distributed in many naval stations.

History is built on intellectual honesty. Often history is reconstructed from wide & varied version of events and old records and these don't come by easily. My initiation and induction in Naval Intelligence department helped me to bring out some hitherto untold facts of 1946 Naval Mutiny in this edition. Outbreak of the mutiny by junior naval sailors was reported to be having political origin and so informed to the British Government in England. A copy of this signal is placed at Annexure I. Political struggles are synonymous with independence and India achieved its Independence shortly after 1946 Naval Mutiny thus bringing an end to further freedom struggles This book appropriately bears the title of 'Untold Story-1946 Mutiny-the Last War of Independence.'

New Delhi   **Lt Cdr G D Sharma, VSM (Retd)**

A Glance at the Sepoy (1857) and Sailors' (1946) Mutinies

	1857 Sepoy Mutiny (First War of Independence)	1946 Sailors Mutiny (Last War of Independence)
Cause of Mutiny	Discontentment in Sepoy Ranks under British Officers	Discontentment in Junior Sailors under British Officers.
Seed of Mutiny	Pig/Cow greased Cartridges.\n\nReligious Overtones (**8 Apr 1857**)	Sub-standard food and unacceptable behaviour of officers. (**Mid Feb 1946**)
Spread of Mutiny	Sepoy Mangal Panday hanged and the mutiny spreads.\n\n(**8 Apr 1857**)	Hunger Strike by Sailors. (**18 Feb 1946**)
Duration of Mutiny	i. **11 May 1857** Delhi captured and Bahadur Shah Zafar enthroned King Emperor of India.\n\nii. **20 Sep 1857** Delhi recaptured and Bahadur Shah Zafar executed by the British. Mutiny continues in other parts of the country and lasted till end of 1859.	**19 Feb 1946-22 Feb 1946**\n\nViolent mutinous acts in all major naval stations across India.
Effects of Mutiny	**2 Aug 1858**\n\nProclamation of British Sovereignty over India	**15 Aug 1947**\n\nIndia attains Independence.

Abbreviations Used

AIR	All India Radio
BOE	Board of Enquiry
CO	Commanding Officer
DNP	Director, Naval Planning
FOB	Flag Officer Bombay
FOCRIN	Flag Officer Commanding Royal Indian Navy
GOC	General Officer Commanding
HM	His Majesty
HMIS	His Majesty's Indian Ship
HMS	His Majesty's Ship
INA	Indian National Army
NHQ	Naval Head Quarters
NAAFI	Naval-Army-Air Force Institute
NOIC	Naval Officer-in-Charge
PRO	Public Relations Office
RAF	Royal Air Force
RI	Rigorous Imprisonment
RIASC	Royal Indian Army Service Corps
RIM	Royal Indian Marine
RIN	Royal Indian Navy
RINR	Royal Indian Naval Reserve
RINVR	Royal Indian Naval Volunteer Reserve
RN	Royal Navy
WT	Weapons Training

1

Birth of the Royal Indian Navy – British Compulsions

Need For Navy

Historical Background

1500 miles of Indian shores are awash by the Indian Ocean. This enormous land mass occupies a prominent position in the Indian Ocean and has nearly 200 small and big ports on its western and eastern coasts. These provided sea links with the other countries of the World. The importance and glory of this geographical prominence is evident from the fact that it is the only ocean in the world to be named after a country, India. It is also a clear pointer that India could have been the hub of sea trade and a thriving maritime power. With abundant natural resources, knowledge of science, the Indian Ocean brought all round prosperity to the entire country. India had excellent relations and booming trade links with all neighbouring countries in the region.

Indian trade with Arab countries extended beyond as far as Egypt. Many Arabs settled in India. They lived in complete harmony with the Indian populace despite their different religion and they inter mingled with the locals. In the flourishing trade, the Arab mariners had control of major sea routes both to the East and the West. The then Brahmanical orders forbade Indian mathematicians and scientists to migrate to foreign lands. Defiance resulted in being ostracized. In fact, the belief of this practice was known to prevail even as late as 1900. India became an insular country taking Himalayas as a protective barrier in the north whilst its southern shores were considered safe and invulnerable to any aggression from the sea.

The Indian Ocean was once a zone of peaceful trade and cross cultural exchanges. It was at the beginning of the end of this tranquillity when in 1498 Vasco da Gama set foot on Indian soil. The ensuing European colonial struggle to gain supremacy in India ultimately resulted in Britain conquering all and thereafter the seas of India remained a virtual British Lake till 1957 when eventually they withdrew from the 'East of Suez' after their colonial rule.

Origin of Royal Indian Navy

From the time of the creation of the East India Company's Navy in 1612 to modern times, the Indian Navy had a history of alternate phases of expansion and reduction when their masters faced emergencies. On the successful completion of assigned tasks, there were subsequent reductions and retrenchments to almost vanishing levels. In a nutshell, the necessity of a navy was more governed by the need of the hour. It did not have any traditions of its own as a fighting force since it was built and trained on the then British pattern of the Royal Navy and also used according to the needs of the times.

During World War I (1914-18), the Indian wing of Navy was styled as 'Royal Indian Marine' (RIM) and had six ships which served as an auxiliary force. Officers of the RIM served at sea with the Royal Navy in multiple theatres of war. They carried out their duties in India, the Mediterranean and East Africa. After Turkey entered the war, the RIM was also employed on river crafts, towing barges to Mesopotamia and other duties in that sector of operations. During World War I, the total strength of the RIM was just 240 Officers, 60 Warrant Officers and 2000 Ratings (Sailors).

After World War I, the Government of India considered many proposals for the reorganization of the RIM. Lord Jellicoe, the then Admiral of the Fleet, the Esher committee and Rear Admiral Mawby who was then the Director of RIM made many recommendations but these were rejected for various reasons. Financial constraints were the over-riding factors. RIM was at its lowest ebb. Another Committee headed by Inchcape further reduced it to little more than a 'Survey Department' and 'Dockyard'. The service then had a sloop named *Clive* for lighting and buoying duties on the Burma Coast where it was also carrying out political duties. Another sloop *Lawrence* was employed for similar duties in the Persian Gulf and *Minto* was the station guard ship at the Andaman and Nicobar Islands. *Cornwallis* and two small ships *Pathan* and *Baluchi* were training ships at Bombay (Mumbai). An old British sloop *Elphinston* was the relief ship. There was a severe shortage of trained officers. With these arrangements, the entire coast of India was guarded by the Royal Navy at a cost of one lac pounds per annum to India.

Rawlinson Committee

In 1925, the Government of India re-appointed a committee for submitting a scheme for reorganising the Naval Service as a combatant force. The chairman was Lord Rawlinson, Minister for Defence in the Indian Government, and the Commander-in-Chief, India were members. The scheme put forward by them was on the lines of the Royal Navy. This force was to have four armed sloops or escort vessels, 2 Patrol Vessels, 4 minesweeper trawlers, 2 survey ships and a depot ship. This was to be set up under the command of a Rear Admiral on active service with the Royal Navy. Recommendations of this committee were accepted both by Government of India and the British Government. *HM* Government also passed an order enabling India to have a combatant navy. The full recommendations of this committee could, however not be carried out without an appropriate and new Indian Naval Discipline Act which had to be passed by both the British Assembly and the Council of State in India. The Act was introduced in 1928 but failed to be passed in the British Assembly. It was again introduced in 1934 with minor amendments and was eventually passed by both the Assembly and Council of State of India. Consequently, the Royal Indian Marine became the Royal Indian Navy on 2nd October 1934 and it was to be modelled on the same lines as the Royal Navy.

2nd October is the date of birth of Mahatma Gandhi, Father of the Nation and an apostle of peace. This date is now universally adopted as the Non Violence Day by the United Nations Organisations. Britain usually neglected the Indian virtues and downplayed Indian character. Could it just be a coincidence or astute British Political diplomacy to procrastinate in deciding the fate of India in this manner? In case it was ever intended to ridicule the non-violent struggle of Mahatma Gandhi for Indian independence, history proved this wrong. The virtual non-violent mass hunger strike by the sailors of the same Royal Indian Navy forced the British Empire in hastening the process of Independence.

The reorganization of the RIM was delayed for a very long time. The circumstances compelled the British Government to decide whether or not to arm the Indian Naval wing and turn it into a fighting force that was solely deployed for harbour duties until then. It must have been a very tough political decision. The changing balance of power in Europe, emerging political activities in India and the British' trust in their own ability to harness these daunting factors to their advantage, was a big challenge to their political acumen. The first and foremost question that would have then arisen was whether it was wise to induct a large number of Indians into an elite defence service and to give them bigger and better weapons especially when the Indian Nation was in a state of political flux and actively indulging in political activities. This political uncertainty and with Communism making an increasing political impact on the peasants and workers of India, it was a likely possibility that these bigger and better weapons might fall in the hands of revolutionaries trained for the cause of Indian Independence. These uncertainties must have weighed heavily with the British Government besides ever present financial constraints and the in built attitude of British superiority against India. The British mind would have wilfully waited and watched for an opportune time for arriving at better bargaining options.

The 'Wait and Watch' British policy was perhaps the best because in the time so gained, concerted efforts were made to bring about alignment of ideas of British democracy with that of the Socialist Republic of Russia and to confront German-Japan fascism. This diplomacy not only pitted the Germans against the Russian military giant but also considerably lessened the impact of Russian Revolution on Indian masses. Communists were even viewed to be supporting British hegemony and lamenting the cause of Indian Independence. In contrast, the Indian National Congress while professing hatred against German-Japan axis was actively organising non-cooperation movements against the British regime and also infusing national spirit in the masses by highlighting past and present brutalities. Their aggressive yet non-violent tactics were earning more moral support from the world over and generating all around sympathy to the cause of Indian freedom. The British government not only responded by forming local self Governments but also made up its mind of transferring power to India soon after the war.

2

Rapid Growth causes Discontent

Wars are fought for furtherance of national and political ideologies or to defend these from the aggressors. In both cases the defence forces serve as the sword arm and are thus shaped accordingly. Both offensive and defensive operations are part of this ideology. At the time of formation of the Royal Indian Navy, India did not have much say in its formation or subsequent development in its growth, on the same pattern as the Royal Navy.

After World War I Great Britain was struggling with its economy. Political realignments and emergence of the Soviet Union were taking place on the European continent. It was thus very likely that the question of re-organisation of the Navy was not to be taken up by Great Britain. India was also intensifying its struggle for independence. In such a critical and complex situation the plan of creating a combatant Navy in India was destined to be delayed for a number of years (1925-1934). It was only when the clouds of war were hovering on Europe; matter was viewed in context with protection of India, a British territory. It is not the scope of this book to focus or highlight details of political situations in Europe or India but the compulsion of circumstances then and travesty of political equations forced the Government of Great Britain to sanction and set up the Royal Indian Navy, on similar lines as the Royal Navy. It then generally became clear that India would also get engulfed in the next World war whose shadows were looming large on the European continent.

The initial setting up of RIN faced an acute shortage of officers and men. For the first time in the Navy a five year plan of expansion was introduced by the Flag Officer Commanding Royal Indian Navy (FOCRIN) in June 1937. As per this plan, there was to be an increase in the number of officers, warrant officers and ratings (sailors). The proposed increase in the strength of personnel was very nominal. It amounted to just, 25 Commissioned Officers, 11 Warrant Officers and 249 sailors. At the end of the war in December 1945, the RIN had 2438 Officers and 21193 sailors, slightly less than a 100 percent increase.

This expansion plan also sanctioned 250 Boys to be inducted into naval service. The 'Boys' cadre was introduced in the Navy for the first time. The Boys Training Establishment (BTE) was set up at Manora in Karachi, now in Pakistan.

Agreement between HM Government and Government of India -1938

The expansion plan was referred back to India for redrafting and review as the expenditure incurred in any one year on the proposed new naval plan could not exceed £100,000 which was the sum hitherto paid to the British government for the defence of the Indian coast. Hence, a new agreement between H M Government and Government of India was formulated in 1938. In this agreement H M Government was to forego the annual subvention of £100,000 and such miscellaneous expenses amounting to £15,000 to £20,000 per annum on condition that the Government of India maintained a sea going squadron of 6 modern escort vessels which would be free to cooperate with the Royal Navy in defence of India and that India would in addition undertake the responsibility of local defence of all Indian ports.

The contribution ceased on 1 April 1938. From these actions it was evident that a world war was imminent and that the British government was arming the Royal Indian Navy for war time duties. Indian political leadership was indignant at these developments but was unable to prevent the growing certainty of India joining the war effort of Great Britain.

Nine Year Expansion Plan

As soon as the 1938 agreement between H M Government and the Government of India was concluded FOCRIN had already worked out a nine year expansion plan to implement this agreement. The plan was examined by the Defence Authority of Government of India and the Admiralty Staff and recommended for approval by the Government. This plan briefly contained these proposals.

(i)   Active service strength of officers and sailors to be increased.

(ii)   Reserve officers and sailors to man auxiliary vessels and defences in war.

(iii) Training cadres for Boys and Apprentices as skilled traders and their induction into active service.

(iv) Five existing sloops to be refitted and armed. One escort vessel to be built.

(v) Six small minesweepers and six motor torpedo boats for harbour defences to be acquired.

(vi) In the event of war, 48 auxiliary vessels would be acquired.

(vii) Training establishments with instructional equipment to be set up at Bombay, Cochin, Vishakhapatnam and sub depots for training of Reserve Officers at Calcutta, Madras and Karachi.

(viii) Provision to be made for the replacement of ships by creating a Sinking Fund.

Chatfield Committee as an 'Expert Committee' examined and approved the nine year plan with minor adjustments.

Administration

Main naval activities centered around naval harbours. Appropriately so, the Naval Headquarters was located at Bombay, now Mumbai. It had six ships and the Naval Dockyard to look after repair and maintenance of these ships and other naval craft. Army was manning Naval Ordnance and Skeleton sea transport. Coastal Batteries for harbour defences were also manned by the Army. Two medical officers from Royal Army Medical corps provided medical cover. All naval affairs at Delhi were looked after by two civilian officers. When reorganisation was taking place, the necessity of placing an officer at Delhi was projected to progress on naval matters requiring professional knowledge. In 1939, an RIN officer was appointed as Liaison Officer for duties in London and Commodore Shewring manned this appointment during the naval mutiny in Bombay.

In the early stages of war, this arrangement was considered adequate and FOCRIN often visited Delhi to coordinate and sort out naval problems. As the war progressed, the arrangement was found wanting. Both operational efficiency of naval ships on sea duties and coordination of naval operations at Delhi for defence of India were the need of the hour. Finally, in March 1941 FOCRIN and Naval Headquarters shifted to Delhi under the War Department of the Government. Though the navy was considered the senior service but the command and control at General Headquarters was under the Army commander.

The general state of service conditions in the RIN and policy programmes were not conducive to good order, naval discipline and efficiency. Adhoc administrative measures were no short cut to laying the foundation of an efficient naval service. The following were very relevant issues:

(a)   Naval Policy

India, a British colony, did not need a permanent combat naval task force. The defence of India was the responsibility of the British Crown. A skeletal marine wing carried out harbour duties. It was only the result of careful and critical analysis of the political situation in Europe and the emerging shadows of war, that the reorganization and expansion of the Royal Indian Marine was finally decided after nearly a decade (1925-34). The basic naval structure of command and control was adapted from the Royal Navy and then in very quick succession 'Expansion Plans' were formulated and approved for implementation. This haste is clearly seen from the fact that before commencement of hostilities the combined strength of the Navy, both Officers and Sailors, was just 1615 but soon after declaration of war in December 1939 the naval strength of personnel was expanded, almost double, and this continued throughout the war.

Earlier, the Indian Naval Dockyard had limited maintenance capacity to provide service to harbour crafts and it could not undertake any new construction. It just provided repair and maintenance services. The induction of war ships to strengthen the newly commissioned Royal Indian Navy was essential, so the old ships of the Royal Navy were inducted and these ships were of mostly of 1924 vintage. The newly groomed Royal Indian Navy with old ships was the replica of the Royal Navy except that these were manned by the newly recruited Indian naval personnel. War time urgencies were very compelling and RIN witnessed a rapid rate of expansion. This can be best appreciated by one simple fact that at the end of the war the total strength of Officers was 2,438 and sailors (Ratings) 21,193 in December 1945 as compared to 1615, both officers and men, before the war.

Every arm of the defence forces, Army, Navy and Air Force has specific roles to perform. Consequently the selection and training of its personnel is also specific and specialized. The role of the naval ship can best be described as, a floating platform, capable of efficiently and effectively propelling itself in all weathers and in all sea conditions and be able to deliver blows lethal to its enemy, be it on land, air or sea and under any weather or sea state whilst adequately protecting itself in these conditions. Earlier, fighting ships had big calibre guns on battleships and heavy cruisers, unlike the present warfare where naval craft are equipped for both offensive and defensive tasks, including a helicopter, for its role at sea.

The selection and training of personnel for these specialised duties is an important all time need in the navy. This was the case when the RIN was being reorganized in 1938-39 but it lacked professional training facilities and the men were given on the job training after 4-6 weeks of a 'Basic and Divisional' course to acquaint them with naval discipline in hastily setup training establishments. The author passed the entrance examination in November 1947 and joined the then premier Naval Mechanical Training Establishment, HMIS *Shivaji* that trained skilled engine room technicians to man and maintain main engines and auxiliary machinery on board naval ships. The men were sent to UK for all other basic and professional courses.

(b)   Personnel – Variable Service Conditions

The complex problem of induction and training of personnel required systematic selection before training but war time contingencies were main constraints. Hence, the personnel were recruited from appropriate professional streams so that they could perform duties on board ships with little naval training. The obvious choice, therefore focused on personnel from merchant shipping companies to fill Indian naval billets.

Uniform service conditions and suitable pay scales for these assorted employees selected from different streams of life but with varying professional naval qualifications were the bone of contention and a burning question. These were always live issues because of differences in age, educational and professional qualifications, practical experience etc. of these employees which were wide and varied. Further, the period of engagement of these men also differed depending upon the scheme of the entry in the service. There were four type of schemes for commissioned Officers, (i) RIN General List officers , (ii) RIN (R) Reserve list officers, (iii) RIN (VR) Volunteer Reserve list officers, and (iv) R N Officers on loan from the Royal Navy. Another cadre of commissioned officers was the Branch List Officers commonly known as Warrant Officers and these were promoted from lower deck, a term used for promotees from the sailors. Their service conditions were altogether different.

The Service conditions for sailors were also not uniform in the Naval service. Besides their professional characteristics, the sailors mainly belonged to two types of service engagement (i) Continuous Service and (ii) Non-Continuous Service. Continuous Service sailors were those who joined service as per peace time recruitment norms. They were generally recruited for 15 years of active service and for varying periods of 'Reserve Service' on completion of active service.

Non-Continuous service personnel were recruited for short periods of duty but their period of employment could be extended on request or requirement of the Service. This was mostly applicable to junior sailors. In the case of senior sailors, with requisite professional qualifications, they were recruited at higher rank and pay for the period of duration of 'Hostilities Only'. This type of entry of sailors into the service was categorized as HO Sailors. They mainly manned Engineering, (both Electrical and Engine Room), and Communication Department/equipment on board ships as well as in the dockyard.

Fixation of pay scales of junior sailors, Ordinary Seaman and Able Seaman, was an uphill task. Majority of their entry was from Private Merchant Shipping Companies and they drew scale of pay fixed by these companies. The basic pay of 'Boy Entry' sailor was Rs 15 per month and it was only peculiar to the RIN. The basic of pay of the Ordinary Seaman in the Navy and their counterparts in the Merchant Shipping Company was Rs 20 per month before the war. After declaration of hostilities an extra 25 percent was added to the pay of Merchant Naval personnel. Those categories of personnel and the HO sailors in the Royal Indian Navy were given an increased basic pay. As the war progressed, their pay scales remained unchanged whilst those who remained in the Merchant Navy were getting war time increments in enhanced proportion. These disparities in their pay fixation remained and were only revised in 1944.

(c)   Desertions

The haphazard induction of personnel and expansion of service adversely affected recruitment targets. Unequal pay scales and bleak chances of promotion in the service coupled with war time risks resulted in frequent desertions from the service soon after enrolment. The magnitude of this problem could be made out from instances when at times the monthly intake of personnel just about balanced desertions. Similarly, the training of the personnel left much to be desired. In 1946 Admiral Godfrey, FOCRIN, told to the Inquiry Commission that since 1940 the Naval Authorities had been taking energetic steps with the Government of India to sanction planned expansion of navy and ship building programmes but they were not forthcoming.. In the absence of any government policy on these important issues, both recruitment of personnel and their training were adversely affected and were the cause of desertions also.

The lackadaisical attitude and slow expansion of naval service during 1939-41 gave a clear edge to the Army to mop up the cream of the population especially in north India. To meet the ever growing requirement of personnel, it was necessary to open recruitment cells on an all India basis, but given the overdrive by the Army, a large number of ratings were enrolled from Bengal and southern states. With the sudden and large intake of personnel, all training establishments had become over crowded. The training staff was also insufficient for the increased work load. It also caused lack of general discipline and disaffection in the service.

(d)   Rosy Picture on Recruitment

During peace time all the three Defence Services were separately recruiting personnel depending on their requirements. Naval recruitment for expansion was sanctioned in 1941. The Navy was ill at ease to meet the sudden demands of personnel. Consequently, a common recruitment procedure for all the services was evolved and it included the services of the local agents. They were paid per capita grant for each recruit that they had brought for enrolment. Posters were published to attract men to join the Navy. Recruiting Officers often painted a very rosy picture of life in the Navy. These lofty promises were found to be hollow in real naval life. There were hardly any promotions as promised at recruitment or published in these posters and this was a resultant cause of discontentment despite the recruitment targets being met. By the end of the war the Navy had 27,651 personnel on its roll against sanctioned strength of 27,706.

(e)   Disparities with other Navies

The Royal Indian Navy was the senior most service but was used for harbour duties. During World War II its role was limited to convoy- cum-escort duties, harbour defences, landing of men and material and manning ferry services in various theatres of war. Occasionally, it had also engaged in gun battles whilst doing these duties. It must be said to the credit of this fledgling service that it acquitted itself admirably in these assigned duties like any professional Naval Fighting Service. Its personnel had earned many awards for bravery and professional excellence in performance of these duties. The deployment of Indian Naval ships in other theatres of war brought their ship companies in contact with men from other Navies and gave them the opportunity to visit other countries. They became aware of service conditions and other benefits afforded to the foreign Navies by their respective Governments. The recreational facility NAAFI (Naval-Army-Air Force Institute) and Canteen Service were available to the naval personnel in all Naval Ports as a morale booster. It provided duty free canteen goods like cigarettes, liquor and other articles. These facilities left an everlasting impression on the men.

The Royal Indian Navy suffered approximately 140 war casualties and about the same number of men wounded in action while performing duties on ships. The Navy also lost six ships during the war.

3

Politics and Political Backdrop

Politics is too complex a subject for the military mind and defence personnel are not allowed to take part in political activities. Although they do not indulge in politics, they do understand different political ideologies as they had lived through political complexities in their regions and states. The scope of this book is not to expound political theories but try to assess its impact on the men joining the armed forces. It is well known that India fought two world wars not because of its own political compulsion but because of the political compulsions of its rulers. India provided vast resources of men and material to augment the British war machine. In both the wars, the threat of internal Indian politics must have caused concern to British authorities and to keep it under check, strict 'Censorship' of the armed forces personnel was instituted. However, soon after the end of World War II Indian naval sailors resorted to mutiny against their own British officers. The wars created areas of disaffection and impacted the mass population in more than one way and it was these men who made inroads into the armed forces.

Demobilization of men after First World War

India was a British colony and it took part in World War I as desired by the British Government. War is not fought free of cost and its heavy expenditure imbalances the economical state of a country. The gloom of price rise, ever-increasing prospects of scarcity cast a shadow all over and shortages were an open invitation to profiteering, black marketing and corruption. Perhaps one may wonder why these negative practices could not be curbed by efficient governance. It is a very tall order as all resources for the security of a country take priority over all other issues. The war adversely affects the economy of a nation no matter how efficient are the political and administrative systems that it operates. During wartime, conditions remain abnormal because it is an inescapable and vital necessity to procure and maintain supply of war goods, at any cost. It in turn compels the manufacturers and suppliers to meet the demand of increased prices and wages of the employee. A chain reaction starts and the worker gradually acquires an increasing sense of power in the sustenance of war supplies. The dictum "Higher Production – Higher profits and hence Higher Wages" strikes a sympathetic chord with all but in turn it makes the economy spiral into a top spin. Under such conditions all the workers belonging to any political group demand better treatment and better amenities of life. In short, it leads to demands from almost all, be they from railways, mines, collieries, farms, factories, tea/coffee estates, commercial firms, corporations, municipal bodies or Government servants without giving adequate returns for money demanded either in skill, quantity or quality.

During World War I Indians were recruited in the armed forces in great numbers and sent abroad to various sectors for war duties. Their educational qualifications were low but service abroad gave them many opportunities to mingle and rub shoulders with soldiers of foreign nations. These casual contacts gave them ample information about their unequal pay and allowances, service privileges and other benefits of war given to them and those given to personnel of British army and troops of other foreign countries. The pay and allowances of these soldiers were higher and their service conditions better than the Indian Army. The rations given to British Indian army were also inferior to their counter parts in other armies. These inequalities might have caused heart burn but did not result in mutiny in the armed forces.

Political aspirations rise and often upheavals follow big events like world wars but Indian politics was then in the formative stage. A strong political pursuit for freedom of the country was at low pitch. "Non-Violence", or passive resistance preached by Mahatma Gandhi was beginning to be adopted and followed by the Indian National congress, the largest multi-religious political party in India. It was not fire branded to snatch freedom for the country and so men in the armed forces might not have been inspired to defy service orders. The subnormal service conditions of the Indian soldiers were known and were the topic of discussion among the Congress leaders. Dr Annie Besant had advocated against joining the war effort on behalf of British Empire but Mahatma Gandhi favoured formation of an ambulance Brigade and sending it to war theatres to help sick, injured and war causalities. This was the best political decision that raised the stature of India and Indian values among the nations of the world and helped to surmount war time recession and inequalities without any breach of discipline.

The Industrial revolution had revolutionized Europe. The process of industrialization was swiftly changing the economical equations in the European subcontinent and significantly altering the balance of power. These conditions were affecting India although India was not directly involved. But one could easily guess the implications for the country in case hostilities broke out between European powers. Germany fully resurrected after defeat in World War I and was aggressively projecting itself as the leader in Europe. The war clouds were gathering fast in Europe and Britain was preparing itself for war time expediencies. It was under these circumstances that proposal for reorganization of the Indian Navy was firstly drawn and then held up for almost a decade (1925-34). When the certainty of war loomed large in Europe, the Royal Indian Navy was not only commissioned in haste but its expansion plan was also sanctioned without any further delay. The war was a topic of general discussion and deliberation amongst Indian political parties and these were now demanding a greater say in governance of the country. Britain, being the past master, placated the political parties by forming 'Local Self-Governments' in various provinces and cleverly obtaining their consensus to support British efforts to fight on behalf of Britain.

The October 1917 Communist revolution against the Tsarist Government in Russia was fast gaining ground and increasing its area of influence in Europe. All East European countries had joined and formed a formidable power bloc in USSR. The impact of Russian revolution and ever growing appeal of communism to masses in India was also considered for liberation of the country by the Communist Party of India. An Indian delegate had participated in International Socialist Congress in Stuttgart where delegates from 25 nations of Europe, Asia (some from Japan and India), America, Australia and Africa were also present. They believed that Proletarian democracy is many times more democratic than any bourgeois democracy. The Communist Party was growing and making rapid progress amongst the peasants and workers. The Indian National Congress and the Communist party of India were for freedom for India. Their aims were the same but their methods differed. One believed in Gandhian non-violence the other advocated direct action to achieve freedom.

Besides political awakening, the effects of European industrialization were also visible in India in raising the aspirations in the masses. The main stream political parties were now sensing freedom from the British yoke. Their political activities were finding prominent place in the press and radio broadcasts and further infusing the spirit of patriotism in the masses. The mammoth anti-British 'Quit-India' movement was aggressively staged all over the country. It may have stirred them but it failed to induce insubordination in the minds of men then in uniform and fighting for the British crown during 1942. The effective isolation of troops in cantonments and fear of strict disciplinary actions by the British high command had kept them away from political activities in the country. Those were anxious days for India when on 3 September 1939 Britain and France declared war against Germany.

World War II --- Politics

The countries aligned themselves due to ideological and political considerations into three groups, Fascist- (Germany and allies as Axis Forces), Democratic- (Great Britain and allies as Allied Forces) and the Combined Socialist Block of Russian Union. There was another group of countries who were not in any power struggle but all the same they had to bear the brunt of war. India was one of such countries that had to go to war on behalf of its rulers. Like World War I it had no choice but to fight on behalf of Britain. Uncertain politics are always hopeful of turning the corner and Indian political parties that were overseeing the liberation of the country devised strategies to achieve this aim. The question of politically compelling and extracting a promise of Indian freedom from the British crown before or during the war would not have been child's play. The winners in war do not part with their conquests and what if Britain lost in war? Indian political leadership was in a strange dilemma to find a satisfactory political solution and convince the Indian masses of any certain assurance of independence of India. The placid British attitude even after failure of 'Cripps Mission' helped both England and India to continue to find an acceptable solution to Independence and Sovereignty of India. In these circumstances the Indian political parties were bartering their support to British war effort.

The Indian National Congress was following this course under the leadership of Mahatma Gandhi and Pandit Jawaharlal Nehru. Their democratic form of Government had roots in the British Parliamentary system. They were working out their strategy to get maximum advantage for their political cause of sovereignty for India. They were not in favour of total Non-Cooperation or rising in revolt but more inclined to build and bring about political pressure. Its 'Quit India' of 1942 was very aggressive. It created hatred for anything imperial and invited strong repressive measures from the Government. This movement stoked passion but it did not kindle the fire of revolt in Indian Defence Forces like that had occurred during the 1857 uprising. The radicals in the party voiced their indignation against supporting British Imperialism and this ultimately resulted in the 'house arrest' of the Congress party leader Netaji Subash Chander Bose. His dramatic escape from custody and foreign sojourns were admired and appreciated by all. His gigantic and unmatchable effort of mobilising Indian Prisoners Of war, forming 'Azad Hind Fauj' (Indian National Army) and fighting against Imperial Forces to liberate motherland India gave a sense and surge of pride to every Indian no matter to which party he belonged to.

The saga of *INA* battle for freedom of India against Allied Forces and planting the Indian National Flag on the soil of India is an ever shining example of the Indian struggle of men in uniform. The cosmopolitan composition of *INA* had overcome religious feelings and they fought as Indian soldiers in uniform. Even during moments of their defeat in war and trials at Red Fort Delhi, the *INA* had uplifted the spirit and march of India to freedom. In 1946, it was this fire and passion for justice that had fanned bickering discontentment into mutiny of Indian Naval sailors against Royal Naval authorities and it helped to hasten the Independence of India. If the 1857 mutiny was 'The First War of Independence', the mutiny of sailors rightly deserves to be remembered as 'The Last war of Independence 'of India.

After the Russian revolution the Communist Party of India had also progressed on the Indian Political horizon. It wielded great influence among Indian peasants and workers. It was active both in villages and urban industrial cities. It was an all India party which urged the people of India to rise like the Russian Revolution to attain freedom from British rulers. Its appeal to the masses was in no way less than the efforts of the powerful political parties, the Indian National Congress and the Muslim League. The success of the Russian Revolution by the peasants and workers against totalitarian regime of Tsars was inspiring.

Politics is a queer combination of seemingly numerous elements. The Indian masses were very impressed by the Russian revolution. The proletarian democracy of Russia was considered better than bourgeois democracy of the west by the Russian Communist Party but both the West and Russia were fighting against Fascist Germany. Muslim League, a politico-religious party was also a powerful player in Indian politics. This was the kind of a perplexing political cocktail when India had helped the British war efforts. An unshakeable rule of British law prevailed in the country throughout the war. There were a few aberrations but to a great extent, good order and service discipline prevailed in Defence Forces and at the end of the war, Indian Military and Naval units took part in the victory celebrations. A few months after the great British victory the discontentment of Royal Indian Naval sailors due to bad service conditions sparked mutiny in the Royal Indian Navy.

After the war, all the political parties were in their own ways making concerted efforts for the independence of India. These varied from the battle against British by the Indian National Army and other covert methods. Notwithstanding these constraints, few political elements were apparently keeping contact with Indian naval sailors in their own ways.

Contact with Political parties

The largest party, the Indian National Congress was disinterested and did not extend any direct support in their naval venture. With independence in sight it advocated for strict discipline in defence forces. The other major party, Communist Party of India, a revolutionary party, must have been disposed to ignite and uphold the rebellious spirit in revolting sailors but it did not directly lead them in their struggle and defiance of authorities. The ratings, political novices, agitating against service conditions, may have assumed their struggle against naval authorities to be like the battle by INA against the British Empire and needing political guidance. In the process some among them might be in contact with political parties and sought their support in their struggle against the naval authority. Likewise political activists would have been also sympathetic to their cause and promised to help them but not openly aligning with their struggle against British Naval authorities. It is a fact that no Indian political leader, like Netaji Subash led the mutinous ratings in their struggle against naval injustice. These sailors struggled without the guidance of political leadership. They were alone in their fight against naval authorities and had to bear the consequences.

Before the mutiny subversive slogans were found written in HMIS *Talwar* and L Tel Dutt was caught with subversive literature. His diary was carefully examined by the Board of Inquiry. In their opinion, his writings leave no room for doubt that he was in touch with some outside organization, the objective of which was to undermine the loyalty of the Forces.

During the investigations it also came to notice that some sailors were visiting some political activists and these contacts preferred to remain in the background. One such activist named Mrs Kusum Nair was examined by the Inquiry Commission and she tendered confusing evidence before the Commission. In her examination before the Commission to the question, "Would you agree if anybody comes in contact with you or your writings would be liable to lose loyalty to the service?" Her answer was, "If they are so influenced, I suppose, they would." To another question, "Are you of the view that it was only on account of the grievances which the ratings had that this strike took place?" Again the answer was non-committal, she said, "I do not have inside knowledge but my view is that it was purely an internal affair and we should give credit or discredit to the ratings themselves for what happened." (In 1971 Kusum Nair supposedly met Mr Hamza Alavi at Michigan University and told him that the mutiny of 1946 was planned to minute details in her home in Bombay. She was a member of the Congress Socialist Party and her husband was a Naval Officer, Pran Nath Nair who later changed to Nayyar and opted for service in Pakistan).

The mill and the dock workers had gone on a sympathy strike in Bombay, Calcutta and other big towns but CPI under the leadership of Shri PC Joshi did nothing to seize the initiative and launch a nationwide struggle. No person from the Communist Party of India had claimed any contact with the sailors but the Mutiny of sailors was a big event. RIN sailors were a fine example of unity especially when India was engaged in the fight for freedom. At this critical juncture, no political leadership, Indian National Congress or Indian Muslim League could have mustered this charismatic unity of sailors belonging to various castes. All political parties sympathized with their cause but none helped or provided direction to them No political party would own responsibility for helping sailors in their agitation against naval authority and would immediately disown any association with them. This was the end result of keeping contact with political parties. The failure of the mutiny by the sailors was a foregone conclusion. The sailors may have been encouraged by political elements in their fight against injustice but they had to bear the consequences entirely by themselves. Their bold action against naval injustice may have brought misery to them but their spirit of defiance of naval authority added perseverance and determination to serve the national cause, at a time when British Government was engaged in negotiations for Independence of India.

World War II was becoming politically inconvenient for Britain to put forth any excuse to undermine the aspirations for complete Indian Independence. While professing to have saved democracy from German Fascism it could not have continued to suppress the spirit of Indian freedom. The mutiny of sailors had added to this spirit and paved the path of *Purna Swaraj*- complete independence. Though the 1946 mutiny was devoid of political leadership this event greatly helped the quest for a better political bargain. It is a fact that Britain advanced the date of relinquishing its rule in India from 1948 to August 1947. It could be to the credit of the mutiny of the sailors that helped hastening the dawn of freedom of India.

Counter Measures

It is wrong to say that defence personnel are immune to politics or political influences which are so openly and widely propagated and practiced in any democratic country. Even before a person joins the Defence Force, he acquires during his school or college time a fairly good knowledge of political practices that are being followed in the country. It is no sin to know about political institutions and various political forces operating in the country. What is forbidden to military personnel is that they are not to take part directly or indirectly in any political activity other than exercising their franchise of voting as per their choice. The apolitical character of men in uniform must be assured at all times. Any deviation from this rigid disciplinary requirement is severely dealt with under the provisions of the Army, Navy or Air Force Acts. These restrictions are generally as follows:-

(i)   Not to be a member or be associated with any society, institution or organisation that is not recognised as part of the Armed Forces of India.

(ii)   Not to be a member or associate with any class of trade or labour union.

(iii)   Not to attend, address or take active part in any meeting or demonstration held by any organisation for political purpose or join any political association or political movement.

(iv)   Not to address electors or publicly announce himself or allow to be publicly announced as a prospective candidate for election to political office.

To ensure strict compliance of these instructions, a professionally skillful and robustly functional investigative organisation called Counter Intelligence Organisation is authorised sanction in defence establishments. Its main duty is to keep strict watch on any political activist or military personnel living in military areas. The activities of civilian Government personnel are kept under watch by the Intelligence Bureau. In short, the subversive activities of any person, whether he is in uniform or a civilian, can be monitored and kept under surveillance in military or in civil area. There is complete cooperation and coordination between civil and military organisations on these issues. Anyone coming to their adverse notice is discreetly kept under unobtrusive surveillance and details of his activities are intimated to the concerned department for further administrative action in the matter. The suspected personnel would also have been kept under watch during 1946 mutiny of sailors, yet some might have escaped their surveillance.

4

Previous Uprisings- State of Discipline during War

Since the advent of civilization countries had been waging wars, usurping land of others and building their own empires. Generally, land borders were easy to cross and the sea borders were considered comparatively safe. Armed sailing ships had been indulging in piracy on the high Seas. The gun fire and mechanization of sailing ships over a period of time enabled sea faring nations to reach out to sea coasts of other countries. The greed of expanding its domain in far off lands thus became a possibility. It was this insatiable British desire to control and rule over far off lands. British diplomacy did the rest and it built an empire of such dimensions that the sun never set on their empire. They conquered nations by a formidable sea force, christened and classified as the Royal Navy, an awe inspiring combatant force having an aura of its own. The Royal Navy maintained this tradition during World War I. Soon clouds of World War II were gathering on the European horizon and the British Government was preparing to meet this threat to protect itself and its far off colonies. The first priority was England and then the rest of their empire. It was such a state of stress and uncertainties during the period 1925- 34 that preceded World War II in 1939.

There were a number of proposals for expansion and reorganization of the Royal Indian Marines for approval by the British Government. RIM was planned to be operational on the same pattern as the Royal Navy. The proposals were rejected or kept in abeyance till such time as the threat of war in Europe assumed serious proportions and became imminent. The British Government was left with no option but to agree and initiate immediate action for reorganization of the Royal Indian Marines like the Royal Navy. RIM was decommissioned and the Royal Indian Navy, (RIN) was formed on 2 October 1934. The requirement of the RIN was considered so operationally urgent and essential that its 9-year programme of phased expansion was also sanctioned soon after its commissioning by the British Government.

Great Britain was arming itself and its territories to fight the oncoming war against Germany. Indian Forces were being strengthened with caution in view of the Indian political struggle for its independence. The Indian National Congress party followed non-violence to achieve its objectives. It required no formal declaration but its righteous sense worked more effectively than any war weapon. World War II was concluded by an atom bomb at Japan killing countless humans but the non-violent non-cooperation killed the soul of British Imperialism and India was freed from the shackles of slavery. The INA trials had fortified the will of the Indian people and the 1946 Indian Naval Mutiny further supplemented the national urge for freedom of India.

The activities of the Communist party were another big challenge to Great Britain. They were also mobilizing and awakening the masses in the struggle for freedom of India. They were politically disillusioned when Russia joined Allies against the Germans. But it did not dampen the spirit of the party and they continued to work for the freedom of the country, often clandestinely, to achieve their objective. This included indoctrination and infiltration into the Armed Forces as well. Usually such attempts were directed to the junior cadres, as the seniors being more ingrained with service discipline, would not be easily susceptible to radical changes. The young junior sailors being disheartened due to bad service conditions and bad behaviour of the British officers were more pliable. The 1946 Indian Naval Mutiny bore such telltale signs of indoctrination. It is a fact that mostly junior cadres of sailors of all branches participated in the mutiny.

There were many incidents of bad food, insulting and degrading behaviour by Royal Naval and Indian Naval Officers, instances of alleged disrespect to religious sentiments and other such irritants that became the cause of a number of minor mutinies in many naval ships and some naval establishments during World War II. Nine recorded mutinies had taken place in the Royal Indian Navy during 1942-1945. These incidents of disobedience or abstaining from food were not of the same magnitude as the uprising of men during the 1946 Naval Mutiny by junior sailors. Lack of discipline among sailors was considered the main reason for these incidents of minor mutinies. Service discipline had always been regarded as an important factor and its compliance was ensured by always keeping all personnel acquainted with its provisions at regular intervals as it automatically instilled fear in their minds. Reading of articles of war is a time honoured practice after weekly divisions (Parades) in the Navy even today.

The definition of mutiny is very frightening. The collective insubordination, the combination of two or more persons resisting or inducing others to resist lawful command of naval authority is termed as a mutiny. Consequences of mutinous acts are punishable with varying terms of rigorous imprisonments. If the act of mutiny is committed with violence it is termed as armed mutiny and the punishment for armed mutiny is death. Just examine its application in normal daily working routine in any naval establishment. Badly cooked food, whether it is due to lack of cooking skill or a bad ration, is required to be complained individually as per the rules. Two persons together and simultaneously complaining about it can be construed as mutiny. This type of irrational orders of inhumane consideration gave rise to loose talk in the mess decks and among men of other departments. The obvious scorn that flows from such conversation lowers discipline, and creates a feeling of disaffection leading to discontentment among the men.

It is normal that during the war, the disciplinary provisions of the Navy Act are regarded as being very stringent and fearsome to ensure a disciplined war machine. The fear of consequences must have helped maintain discipline in the armed forces during the war time. It could perhaps be as well a reason that the minor mutinies during the war did not snowball into major incidents of indiscipline or mutiny by the naval personnel. The main reasons of indiscipline among men during these mutinies were mainly attributed to mass recruitment and hasty initial training of personnel during the war. The failure of discipline was due to insufficient and inefficient training as it did not inculcate discipline in men to the desired level. In 1940, at the very beginning of the war, some inconsequential and minor mutinous acts were noticed in HMIS *Bahadur* at Karachi and Castle Barracks at Mumbai. These continued at various other places during the war. Summaries of these incidents of minor mutinies during 1942-45 war are enumerated in the succeeding paragraphs.

3 March 1942, Mechanical Training Establishment (MTE) Bombay
Apprentices did not get an increase in the pay but war messing allowance of Rs 5-7 paid to them was also deducted from their pay.

Seven apprentices were tried by court martial for mutiny, disobedience and breaking out of barracks and sentenced to 3-15 months imprisonment. They were released before completion of their sentence as the active service of apprentices only starts to be counted after completion of training. Their Divisional Officers had prior knowledge of this 'strike' as they were told about the plan of action. The concerned officers were censured by FOCRIN.

22 June 1942, HMIS *Konkan* at Tobermory, UK 17 ABs/ODs(Able body and Ordinary Seaman) refused to work or obey orders and resorted to a hunger strike. They had requested for better scale of ration, issue of milk and butter. They had also complained about very long working routine, inadequate arrangements for sleeping, and no radio facility for Indian news or Indian programmes. It was their simmering discontentment over a period of time that took the form of mutiny on 22 June when fresh bread was not available for breakfast. 'Atta' issued for chapattis was old, musty and with weevils. The disparity in their ration, working routines and pay in comparison to service conditions of the Royal Naval ratings and their working conditions caused discontentment. The ships officers ignored and treated these as minor complaints. There was no outside influence but 4 sailors assumed leadership. In all 17 sailors were sentenced to 90 days detention and dismissed from the service.

September 1942, HMIS *Orissa* at New London South Africa There was hardly any communication and complete lack of discipline as there was no contact between officers and their men. The ship had no officer on board at night except a Norwegian Engineer officer who was unable to communicate and make him understood to the men. **On the night of 16 Sep 1942, there was disturbance in a hotel between the Manager and the Indian ratings on account of colour bar and 9 sailors were arrested.** The next day, the ship's company refused to surrender their out passes when ordered to do so by the Executive Officer. The Commanding Officer, Executive Officer and Gunnery Officer were tried by Court Martial and punished with loss of seniority. **Three sailors were tried by Court Martial for mutiny with violence and sentenced to 3-7 years imprisonment.** 13 sailors were also punished with loss of their rank.

September 1942, HMIS *Khyber* at U K

 (a) 6-7 greasers refused to carry out messenger duty stating that it led them to being ostracized.

 (b) 15 men had complaints against the chief, Bosun Mate. (Head of Seamen sailors)

 (c) Engine Room ratings showed complete lack of technical knowledge.

 (d) Asdic Sailors refused further training.

 (e) 6 Sailors refused sentry duties.

 (f) Seamen sailors refused painting the ship.

 (g) Four rifles were lost and there was scurrilous writing on the wall of the building housing the ship's company.

A Board of Inquiry was held. The ship's company was found to be professionally inadequate and ill-disciplined. Most of the crew was from Chittagong and future recruitment from there was reduced to a minimum. The dock authority warned that in case of such an inefficient crew being deputed again, the ship will not be delivered to the RIN by the Royal Navy. Three sailors were dismissed and no action was taken against the greasers.

27-28 June 1944, HMIS *Akbar* at Bombay There was mass disobedience by 100 ratings (80 per cent of the ring leaders were Pathans from the North West Frontier) on religious grounds. They refused to sweep the mess deck stating that it was against their religious practice. They had demanded building of a mosque for prayers and some other religious facilities soon after their arrival.

Hundred ratings were discharged and the recruitment of men (Pathans) with such traits was restricted. Drug addicts or those not amenable to good discipline were also not to be recruited.

30 July 1944, HMIS *Hamlawar* A sailor of Leading seaman rank put in a request in a proper service manner that while he was reading the 'Quran', an officer struck him on his back because he had not responded to his question "Where is Dil Hussain?" Interruption of prayers is an insult to his religion. Other Muslim ratings sympathized with his cause and bodily assaulted this officer.

Board of Inquiry was constituted. The Officer made a public apology at Divisions on 3 August 1944. He was tried by Court Martial, severely reprimanded and deprived of three months seniority. 13 sailors were also tried by Court Martial and sentenced to various terms of imprisonment for violence against the officer.

29-31 July, 1944 HMIS *Shivaji* 17 Muslim ratings refused food stating that the mutton was contaminated with the meat of the pig. Later an impartial inquiry into the complaint found it to be false. These men were discharged on the same day after permission from higher authorities. Next day two more sailors had a similar complaint. They were reassured and the complaint was withdrawn. Again on 31 July, 26 ratings complained that they could not eat any kind of food cooked in the galleys. The complaint was investigated impartially. All except four took the meals and returned to work. 4 were summarily discharged from the service.

16 March 1945, *HMIS Himalaya*, Karachi 3 Leading Seamen requested to go to the mosque for Friday prayers. On the refusal of permission they broke ship. They were tried by Court Martial and sentenced to one year imprisonment.

17 April 1945 *HMIS Shivaji* 51 direct entry ratings of all religions refused to clean their living places saying it is against their religion. A Committee of officers found it to be more on account of dissatisfaction with the conditions in the service. 44 ratings were given 90 days RI and removed from the service.

It is appropriate to make mention of a letter dated 23 April 1945 from Commander Coverdale, the then Commanding Officer of *HMIS Shivaji* reporting this incident. In this letter he stated, "I am convinced that the refusal to clean the ship is mainly an expression of disaffection on their part (Men) with the terms and conditions of service about which they were misinformed. The disaffection coupled with their feelings that higher authority is not going to consider their grievances, which they know have been frequently represented officially by letter and also placed before the committee of inquiry convened. Their state of mind is such that they are prepared to go to jail rather than pinning any further faith in possible redress of their grievances by the higher authorities".

It was not that the higher naval authorities had only ignored this report in April 1945 from *HMIS Shivaji*, but even before too, the naval authorities took no cognizance of such grievances in the Navy. There were a number of such situations with a variety of disaffection in men that had impinged upon the minds of the men and the naval officers in those stressful war times. Under war conditions, it was just that both the officers and the men were biding their time and running the naval show hoping for some miracle to ease their tension.

In January 1943, the then FOCRIN Vice Admiral Fitz Herbert felt so alarmed that he circulated a cautionary note to all the Commanding Officers to remind them about the famous saying of Napoleon, "There are no bad men, there are only bad officers." He implored all officers to be more responsive and stressed the need for intelligent and tactful handling of men under their command. He decreed that the practice of officers always taking the first opportunity of leaving the ship on arrival in the harbour is to cease. They should leave the ship only if there was no work or no men in his Division had any need for his assistance or advice. The practice of officers boarding last on the boats going ashore from the ships is even followed till date in all Indian Naval ships. Admiral Fitz Herbert was replaced by Vice Admiral John H Godfrey who was then serving as Director of Intelligence at Admiralty in London.

With regard to the curbing of disaffection arising from religious incidents, Admiral Godfrey FOCRIN in April 1945 issued guidelines to all naval authorities that it is their duty to give reasonable facilities to the men under them to perform their religious duties. These instructions allowed freedom of religion but propagation of religion was not allowed. This policy helped maintain religious harmony among the men. As the date of independence was nearing, grouping of men of same religion were noticed but there was no untoward incident because of religion. The religious divide amongst men in uniform was unnoticeable although communal disturbances were taking place in some parts of the country. In those circumstances, the sailors mutiny in 1946 was a shining example of religious harmony amongst the naval sailors and all men in uniform. There were hardly any differences on account of division of defence assets on the partition of India.

5

Organization and Administration in Navy

"Those who play the game do not see it as clearly as those who watch it" a Chinese proverb is undoubtedly a gem of wisdom but it puts great responsibility on the person watching the game for an objective and unbiased review of events as also having a discerning eye for details and in-depth knowledge of the subject matter. The correct description of the RIN mutiny without these requisites would not do justice to the spirit of the mutiny of the sailors in 1946. The explicatory description of the origin of the RIN, its organizational and administrative factors give a fair background of the 1946 mutiny of the sailors. These organizational and administrative measures, so devised to command and control the men were the backbone of the naval discipline but it failed.

OFFICERS

In 1939, the strength of officers in the RIN was 212, about 20 percent were Indian and 80 percent were British Officers. By 1945, their total strength rose to 2852. Of these, 1377 were British, 949 Indian, 249 Anglo Indians and 70 officers from other nationalities were on the active list. Throughout the war, the higher ranks in the Service and the important administrative posts in the Navy were held by British and Europeans officers. These officers always held an air of superiority. The highest ranking Indian officer at the end of the war was Lieutenant Commander HMS Choudri, who opted for service in Pakistan after partition.

SAILORS - Organisation and Professional Duties

The ship is an independent and composite fighting unit carrying out specific types of naval duties on the high seas. In World War II, the ships of the Royal Indian Navy were mainly deployed for escort, mine sweeping and harbour duties for which these ships were suitably designed and equipped.

The main branches of sailors corresponded to type of their professional departmental duties on board ships. There are three cadres in the navy-Executive, Engineering and Supply and Secretariat now known as Logistics. The Executive department consists of Seamen sailors who look after ship's husbandry and man gun quarters. The Engineering department comprises of Marine Engineering and Electrical Engineering. The skilled technicians, Artificers and technically less qualified sailors of these branches known as Stokers (MEs) and E Ms maintain machinery on board ships. The Supply and Sectt branch is combination of Writers (Clerks), Store Assistants, Cooks, Steward and Topasses (Sweepers). The specially trained sailors from Executive cadre, Communications branch, carry out wireless and signal communication duties on board ships. Comparatively, these sailors are well-informed and class apart from other seamen. It was sailors from communication branch who were first involved in the 1946 mutiny in the navy.

The basic education for entry in the service was Matriculation for Artificer Apprentices and Communication Sailors. For all other branches, the basic education qualification was Non Matriculation. The professional training of the sailors was carried out in their respective Training Establishments but sailors of all branches undergo the Basic and Divisional course for approximately three months duration. It is an introductory course to naval life and teaches Naval Organisation, Parade and Field Training and acquaints men with Service Conditions and Naval Discipline. There were three pay scales- matriculates were in 'A' pay group and non-matriculates in 'B 'pay group but Cooks, stewards and topasses were in 'C' pay group. The rank structure of the sailors was Leading hand, Petty Officer and Chief Petty Officer in their respective branches. These ranks corresponded to Naik, Havaldar and Jamedar respectively in the Army but Chief Petty officer, unlike in the army, was a non-commissioned rank in the Navy. The Navy and Air Force did not have Viceroy Commissioned officers or as now known Junior Commissioned Officers. The Navy had the rank of Warrant Officer that was peculiar to this Service. Warrant Officer was also regarded as a commissioned rank officer but not equated with King Commissioned granted to all regular officers of the three Defence Services. Warrant Officers had a separate mess and were promoted from the select cadre of Chief Petty Officers with exceptional service record over a very long period of time. The rank of Warrant Officer in the navy was discontinued in 1963. In a nutshell, this was the composition of the sailors in the naval service but only Sailors of Leading and below ranks of various branches had taken part in the 1946 mutiny.

The strength of the sailors in 1939, at the beginning of the war, was 1475 and it rose to 21193 in 1945 by the end of the war. These men belonged to various castes and were approximately in the following proportion during period 1939-1945:-

	1939	1945
Hindus	9 .25 %	42 .50 %
Muslims	75 %	35 %
Christians	13 %	19 .50 %
Sikhs	0.25 %	2 %

There were 2 percent Anglo Indians and the remaining was from other miscellaneous castes.

Before the outbreak of World War II, the majority of the sailors belonged to Punjab, Bombay coastal areas, and a small percentage was from the NWF Province, Madras-Travancore-Cochin and Goa/Portuguese coastal areas with very small representation from Bengal, Bihar/Orissa. At the end of the war, percentage of sailors was approximately- Punjab 20%, Tranvancore and Madras 34 %, Bengal-Bihar-Orissa 13%, Bombay 8.25 %, UP and Central India 12 % with a sprinkling of sailors from the other provinces of India.

The life of sailors on board ships was very tough. There was scarcity of space, generally the sleeping space was just for the two-third strength of a Ship's Company and the one-third was supposedly to be on duty manning the ship. There was always a shortage of water, clank-clank of machinery and weariness due to rolling and pitching of ship caused sea sickness which was taking its own toll. At times in rough seas, cooking food in the galley was the severest test of human endurance. It sounds terrible but the situation must have been horrible on board ships in mid-thirties when the ships were of old design and propelled by old slow moving reciprocating engines consuming steam at a rate that was just about its maximum distilling capacity of water needed to raise steam for the machinery. Fresh water was in perpetual scarcity on board ship. These privations and hardships in day-to-day life together with bad food or other service conditions was the life of a juniors sailors at sea. It is another amazing feature of naval life that the rigours of sea life fade out very soon from memory on seeing or setting foot on land. The personnel quickly revert to their usual professional duties and carry out normal daily routine of scrubbing and cleaning their Mess Decks and living spaces. The life of the sailors in the shore establishment was comparatively much healthier, peaceful with regular working hours. The communication sailors were deployed for a four hourly watch keeping duty in WT offices and manning WT stations for 24 hours on all days.

Service Discipline

The introductory 'Basic and Divisional course' which a sailor undergoes on entry into the service trains him for service drills, instils service discipline and moulds a raw recruit into sea-going sailor. Naval discipline not only restricts or curtails various civil liberties but also lays down guidelines for personnel to conduct themselves in a proper service manner while carrying out their assigned naval duties. Naval discipline directs that any complaint regarding service matters must be made individually even if it is of common cause and affecting other personnel in a similar manner. This simple but very effective technique routinely isolates and segregates personnel voicing common grievances. It will be appreciated that this order does not allow collusion between men with the same complaint and does not allow the situation to develop into a common cause mass discontentment though all of them may have the same grievance against the naval service. This type of simmering discontentment amongst them if not detected and corrected, may eventually lead to subversive acts and defiance of naval authority. No administrative authority would like such a situation to ever arise or develop into a group or mass agitation in his command.

Indiscipline- Security Risk

The sheer negligence in administration coupled with continuous bad service conditions could result in inducing men to resort to illegal agitation that often starts with loose talk in the mess decks. The fear of discipline will not drive them to open defiance of naval authority or inspire anyone of them to assume the role of leader in an open agitation against the faltering administration. Under these conditions mistrust between men grows in the mess decks and some elements are suspected of being informers. The veil of secrecy and witch hunt is constantly feared by those who indulge in any subversive activities. The fear of serious disciplinary action deters them and the fear of being exposed curbs the spirit to lead an open agitation.

Under these deceitful and fearsome circumstances the ring leaders may endeavour to induce others to voice common cause grievances collectively. In this state of affairs, though silently willing to spearhead the movement but the lack of courage hinders someone to lead from the front. Due to lack of courage to openly violate service rules, effort is thus made to seek help and guidance surreptitiously from local political elements. After World War II, the political parties may also have found it expedient and politically gainful to extend help to the agitating sailors.

Naval discipline must have been under considerable and constant strain during the war due to bad service conditions. The threat to service discipline would have further increased on account of political strife like the 'Quit India' movement. The naval administration had lived through a number of hunger strikes during the war. Yet it was unable to stem the discontent of the men and in February 1946 after the war when sailors of HMIS *Talwar*, a Communication Training establishment, staged a hunger strike which quickly spread to other naval stations. Undoubtedly, not only bad service conditions and unjust naval administration but also an uncertain future had upped the ante and infuriated all personnel awaiting demobilization after the war. Their discontentment must have been very high as they were left with no hope of getting their rightful dues before bidding goodbye to the service. It was the right recipe to stir them up for defiance of naval orders to pave the way for mutiny. The political elements would like to misuse and exploit these circumstances. Service personnel normally do not like to mingle with political elements or to take risky initiatives by themselves but some of them might have been in contact with them to voice service grievances for help for action by the naval authorities.

The clandestine contact with political elements may not be merely limited to espouse the grievances but also to highlight these by resorting to widely circulating these grievances amongst their other colleagues. This is how the men are cleverly guided to the next stage of a silent agitation. These select few were quietly confided with the task of writing anti-service graffiti on mess decks or common places and to organize distribution/ circulation of leaflets and pamphlets in ships and establishments. Such activities resulted in loose talk in other places thereby leading to the acts of collective indiscipline, boycott and strikes, whilst the ring leaders remained incognito. It was in such conditions and a chance coincidence that pointed the finger of suspicion at L Tel B C Dutt when some leaflets were found during a search of his locker. Hunger strike is more appealing to forge unity among agitating personnel. Collective passive resistance inadvertently boosts the morale of agitating men, forging unity, encouraging them to defy authority which leads them to the state of mutiny. The 1946 mutiny followed the same pattern.

In the diplomatic quagmire of politics then practiced in the country in 1946, the mutiny of sailors was an issue that could hardly be ignored by any political party, especially the parties that believed in armed struggle to reach power and the Communist Party of India had strong belief in the principles of Russian revolution. The other major political parties, Indian National Congress and Indian Muslim League were nonchalant about the uprising of the sailors. The Congress advocated non-violence and the Muslim League wanted a separate state for the Muslims of India. The struggle of the sailors was without political guidance. Perhaps these political parties were engaged in higher strategies and courses of action for sovereignty and liberation of India from the British Crown.

Morale and Security Reports

Preserving and maintaining a high standard of discipline in all naval units had always been a very important factor for efficient naval administration. The Commanding Officers of all Naval Ships and Establishments were then and now also required to render morale and security reports to Naval Headquarters on all men under their command. These reports included any untoward incident or any peculiar trend observed in men on board ships/establishments. The Department of Personnel in the Naval Headquarters meticulously processed these reports and suggested suitable remedial actions whenever any adverse activity came to their notice .The Department of Personnel in the Naval Headquarters in Delhi was then headed and manned by the army officers.

The Navy had 44 Ships and establishments in India and at Aden. All these units rendered morale and security reports to NHQs. Adverse observations were known to have been made in these reports but no remedial action followed. Consequently, in spite of these reports no suitable administrative action were initiated and as a result break down in discipline followed and the mutiny overwhelmed almost all ships and naval establishments in the country and Aden. The magnitude of the resultant naval mutiny involved almost all junior sailors except those who were then borne on the following ten ships/ units. Of these ten units, five were not stationed in India or in Indian waters then.

HMIS *Shamsher,* a frigate in Bombay harbour.

HMIS *Dilawar,* Boys Training Establishment at Karachi.

HMIS *Godavari* at Madras.

HMIS *Barracuda* at Calcutta.

HMIS *Tir* at Vizagapatnam.

HMIS *Investigator* and HMIS *Llanstephan* at Trincomalee, and

HMIS *Kaveri*, HMIS *Sutlej* and HMIS *Calcutta* at sea in the Pacific

Though incidents of minor mutinies were reported during war and collective punitive actions were also taken against personnel but it did not flare up in mutiny at these naval stations. The morale and security reports pertaining to the period May-July 1945, just before the end of World War II, showed no abnormal activity. The end of the war was a very jubilant event. Whilst all would heave a sigh of relief but political ambitions for the freedom of India were also intensified. These reports did not sound any alarm and were considered normal. Generally, these reports indicated that:-

(a) Morale of the men was very high. A sense of achievement was noticeable in the euphoria of victory. British personnel were keen about elections in England whilst Indian personnel were keenly looking to the 'Wavell Proposals' and how it would shape India.

(b) No subversive activity or incident of leaflets / pamphleteering was reported, and

(c) No noticeable reaction to newspaper reports was reported.

These reports clearly indicated that all naval personnel were maintaining a high standard of naval discipline and there was no abnormality in their behaviour on any account. Morale and security are not casual returns but are always rendered with utmost care and caution. The very purpose of these reports is to acquaint the higher command on current issues and activities pertaining to service conditions, political, social or religious issues lest these may not result in disaffection among the personnel leading to discontent amongst them. Discontentment is the first step to subversion which when neglected results in clandestine and unlawful activities and undermines discipline in the service. Subversive elements, be they from any political party, religion or any foreign organisation, are always known to be discreetly contacting disgruntled/discontented men in uniform to further their influence. It requires painstaking tactful observations and prudent skills to handle such elements. Correct assessment is a highly sensitive and delicate task. It undoubtedly requires constant and discreet observations to assess and render these reports. It is a fact that the morale and the security reports failed to foresee and forecast the indiscipline in men shaping into the 1946 mutiny.

The morale and the security reports are often found wanting in assessment and not projecting alarmist reports on any sensitive issue in units. Unit resources are inadequate and there may be hesitation to delve deep into stray and unpleasant incidents. The outlook of an officer rendering morale and security reports is also a factor, because any adverse observation might impinge on the reporting officer too. It is, therefore, important that breaches of discipline be viewed with an open mind and reported. The acts of indiscipline in any unit are bound to be a sad reflection of its Commanding Officer. Consequently these reports may be watered down whilst reassuring superior authorities that adequate care and caution is being taken to defuse the cause and that the situation is under control. In naval parlance it reads as "keeping your yard arm clear". There was a clear divide between the senior and junior rank ratings in HMIS *Talwar*, the birth place of the 1946 mutiny, on account of bad service conditions but it went unnoticed and unreported. The officers and senior sailors failed to gauge the mood of junior sailors under them. These local administrative shortcomings were not reflected in the morale and the security reports. It was only the ratings of Leading rank and below, from all branches that organised the mutiny but no senior rank sailor, petty officers or Chief Petty officers, did not even know about it although it was their duty to keep themselves fully informed of any unrest in lower mess decks.

It was not a great surprise that the morale and security reports for August, September and October 1945 from all ships and establishments were fairly normal despite the fast changing political climate in the country. The news regarding the Indian National Army and it trials for treason were sweeping the whole country. These reports must have impacted naval units but morale and security reports from all naval establishments were satisfactory and did not reveal any bad influence or any undercurrent or subversive activity amongst the sailors. It was the same case with report from HMIS *Talwar*, the birth place of the February 1946 mutiny. With regard to HMIS *Himalaya*, the Training establishment at Karachi where violent action took place, the Morale and Security reports merely mentioned that the grouse, in the messes of ratings and information/reading rooms, where periodicals and newspapers were available, was that these newspapers were either sponsored or only supplied by the officers or Naval Headquarters. In an earlier report from this establishment it was mentioned that there was no newspaper in Karachi that does not try to create discontent against the British rule. It also mentioned that there may be political disagreements in Hindu and Muslim personnel but both favoured Independence of India. All was thus apparently normal as per these reports. In a nutshell, the summary of Morale and Security reports from Karachi was that:-

(a) There may be differences in the men but they presented a united strategy in favour of Independence of India. Silently, Hindu sailors were in sympathy with Indian National Congress and Muslim sailors supported Muslim league.

(b) The interest of the ratings was enlivened by the cause of the Indian National Army.

(c) Large coverage of INA trials by the press had definitely swayed the ratings and evoked political consciousness in all. Some sailors even subscribed to the INA Relief Fund. Some officers and majority of ratings were sympathetic to INA though not associated with their activities.

(d) All officers and educated sailors read newspapers and associated propaganda therein but there were no pamphlets or leaflets in any of the Naval Establishments.

In the past, bad service conditions and religious sentiments had caused mutinies in the Navy but unlike in 1946 these failed to spread to other units of the service. Graphic details of the political situation in the country with its likely impact on service personnel, the sudden spurt in recruitment to meet war time emergencies, lack of training and ill discipline were already known to the naval authorities. *What really then changed so radically after the war in the Naval Service which caused defiance of authorities in many ships and naval establishments across the country and shook the roots of British Imperialism despite ever widening religious fissures in Indian society?*

6

Causes of Discontentment

An unjust law is itself a species of violence. Arrest for its breach is more so.

- MK Gandhi

An unjust system of governance thrives on unjust policies and practices of its administration. It was no secret that the British Government was expanding and arming the newly formed Royal Indian Navy on the pattern of the Royal Navy to supplement its own war efforts to fight a fast approaching World War. All aspects whether the newly constituted Navy should follow the same type of naval law and administrative rules applicable to the Royal Navy including their service conditions were the question. It must have been a sensitive issue with the Admiralty in England as to whether these be the same as in the Royal Navy. The equality in service conditions of both RN and Royal Indian Navy could never have been the same and these were bound to be very much different. The service conditions for Indian Personnel, whether they pertained to pay and allowances, food, scales of ration, rail travel, leave, accommodation, medical and host of other administrative daily functions on board ships and establishments were different. The British officers acted like demigods and their bad behaviour smelt of the 'Racial Discrimination'. The stress and strain of war had awakened the Indian masses. The saga of the Indian National Army and its fight against British rule stirred Indian patriotism. British aura had declined after the war. The simmering discontentment of men during the war had made them restive due mainly to bad service conditions and increased political activities in the country were helpful to the agitation against naval authorities. The main irritants that caused discontentment were as given below.

(a)   Misrepresentation at the time of recruitment

It was not only the need of the jobless youth of India to seek employment in Naval Service but it was also an essentially urgent and immediate necessity of Britain to recruit personnel for manning the expanding role of the Royal Indian Navy. The Recruiting Offices manned by army personnel were recruiting personnel but there was no uniform policy for enrolment of men. The Recruiting Offices were also sending recruitment parties to areas under their charge to enrol personnel for the Navy. These parties had no uniform instructions and gave widely varying versions of Naval Service conditions to new recruits. Although misrepresentation of naval service conditions by them was not the primary cause of the mutiny but a large number of ratings mentioned this as a grouse against the Service. Their evidence hardly left any doubt that they were given false assurances of pay and allowances, promotional prospects and resettlement employments after the war. In fact in one of the naval ships refusal to clean ship causing a mutiny on board was because of this misrepresentation. The evidence of many men before the Inquiry Commission was irrefutable and found to be true. Many type of recruitment material was examined. It included 'recruiting posters, pamphlets', and various other official documents available at Naval Headquarters. These documents clearly reflected intention of misrepresentation and misinformation about naval service to attract men to the navy to fulfil its immediate requirements. These official documents amply supported evidence of men but they were still punished.

This was the statement of Rear Admiral Rattray, Flag Officer Bombay (FOB) before the Inquiry Commission. He said, "The average rating firmly believed that he was going to be provided post war job by the Service. The Government and the Navy cannot be held blameless for this. Much of the recruiting advertising was literally on the lines, 'Join the Navy and secure yourself a post war job.' Admittedly though no such promise was in the text of advertisement but the caption certainly implied that." Even quarter ending reports of Morale and Security dated 31 December 1945 to Naval Headquarters mentioned that the men had complained of false promises on recruitment but were being sent out without any provision of employment in civil life.

The statement of FOB was a of general nature but Commodore Lawrence, Staff Officer Operation at Naval Headquarters (1939-end 1941) submitted many recruiting posters, pamphlets and booklets to the

Commission of Inquiry and stated that these contained promises that tried to encourage people to believe them but these are not quite as they would have been. Generally posters and pamphlets painted rosy pictures of prospects being offered to attract men to volunteer for enrolment. A sample of a recruitment booklet would have conveyed to an aspirant of jobs in the Navy. It was titled 'The Navy and its Job'. It stated that the Royal Indian Navy is moulded on the lines of the Royal Navy because without exception the Royal Navy is the oldest, most efficient and finest fighting service in the world. It further states that India's Navy is growing fast. It needs to grow faster if security is to be ensured. The Navy needs men of intelligence and singleness of purpose who united, will man India's warships and protect India's sea borne trade against the aggressor. The contents of the booklet pepped up Indian nationalism in sailors while elucidating superiority of the Royal Navy. Any Indian in British government service, including the Recruiting Officers and their Propaganda units could not have dared to overtly or covertly try to arouse Indian nationalism. The war time naval administrative machinery had no time to think and assess the consequences of their hollow promises. Truly the representation and publicity for recruitment of personnel was grossly misleading and false. It was nothing but deliberate attempt to deceive and to lure new recruits to join the RIN to strengthen the British war effort.

(b)　　Food – Source of serious discontentment

Bad quality of food served to Royal Indian Naval ratings was the commonest grievance voiced by almost all. The bad food routinely served in the naval service had become the immediate cause that generated and spread anti-service feelings among the men. Bad quality food acted as a catalyst which slowly became catastrophic and created conditions which were beyond the comprehension of the newly appointed Commanding Officer of HMIS *Talwar*. It soon turned into disobedience and spread to many ships and establishments giving out a signal for mutiny in the naval service.

Food, no doubt, had been an essential requirement to maintain good order and discipline in the armed forces. Unwholesome and unpalatable food caused a nauseous feeling of disgust and self pity when no efforts are made to improve the quality of food. This is the first stage of discontentment in men. In case such conditions continue to prevail over a period of time the administrative inaction become talking points among men bringing out anti-service feelings in them. This situation is surely not conducive to good administration. That Bad food created unrest among the ratings of HMIS *Talwar* is abundantly clear from heaps of evidence brought out during the inquiry. There were many instances of outbreak of serious indiscipline during war due to bad food. The constraints of war, perhaps, had muffled these from blowing into alarming crises. It is even not arguable that men in bitterness against their superior officers might have over stressed bad quality of food. It may, however, be feasible that service discipline and strains of war may have hardened them to bear with these bad service conditions and that the quality of food would improve after the war. It was a fact that when the war ended, the quality of food did not improve but went from bad to worse. Bad quality of food had thus become a rallying point and important factor of unity among all sailors. The result was hunger strikes by men and it ultimately paved the way for open mutiny in HMIS *Talwar* which thereafter spread to almost all naval ships and establishments of the Royal Indian Navy.

(c)   Rations and supply system

The main supplies for food in the Navy then were, atta, and flour, rice, dal (pulses), meat, vegetables, and condiments. Each one of these articles was a subject of complaint but more prominent being atta, flour, rice and vegetables.

Till 1941, the Navy obtained ration supplies directly from its own contractors chosen for their reliability, dependability and competitive prices. All supplies were checked and bad items were rejected then and there. The threat of cancellation of their contract had ensured immediate remedial effect and so the quality of all rations was always maintained. Financial and economical constraints, late payments due to war, adversely affected this arrangement as also quality of victuals. Concurrently, demands also increased due to unprecedented expansion of the defence forces. The delivery to ships became arduous and erratic. There was a noticeable fall in the quality of rations supplied by contractors. Difficulty in procurement and ever increasing demands of the Navy necessitated that the supply of rations and stores to all defence services be centralized. After due deliberations and discussion in the war department the supply of all ration stores for the Navy was entrusted to the Royal Indian Army Service Corps (RIASC) on 1 April 1943. The new arrangements did not bring about any improvement in the quality of rations but instead it further deteriorated in course of time.

The Food Department of the Government, for Civil Supply System was constituted soon after the war. It consisted of Directorate of Food Inspection for procurement of ration supplies for civil distribution. Initially, this Directorate had followed RIASC standards. In July 1943 it was entrusted with the duty of supplying rations to the Defence Forces also. The demands for rations were continuously increasing due to the ever increasing strength of the Armed Forces but procurement of ration stores was slowing down and steadily decreasing. The supplies totally got cut off from Burma after Japanese occupation. The procurement and inspection of victuals was becoming an onerous task. The Food Department delegated the responsibility of procurement of ration supplies to the State Governments and their inspection and grading had to be accepted although RIASC was still inspecting these supplies before issue to Defence Forces and it became a bone of contention. The tolerance of state Governments regarding foreign matters, namely paddy, grit, dirt, earth particles etc were much higher than that of RIASC. As applicable to the state of 'Central Province and Berar' it was between 2 to 0.5 % and it was much higher than the tolerance set by RIASC. It was this type of arrangement under which consignments of victuals with higher impurities were supplied and had to be accepted. RIASC was getting supplies under this system and was further issuing these to Base Victualing Officers of the Royal Indian Navy for distribution to ships and establishments under their own arrangements.

(d)   Base Victualling Organisation of RIN

The RIASC was procuring supplies for the Navy, therefore the duties of Base Victualling Officers of the Navy were to liaise with RIASC for procurement of supplies. They were to acquaint themselves with local supply conditions, deal with any complaint from the Ships/Establishments and ensure that the stores were timed for within warranty period. As per rules and then prevailing practice, acceptance of supplies from RIASC under warranty period had to be accepted. All supplies had therefore to be examined and verified for quality and quantity before signing an acceptance. It thereafter clearly implied that the receiving officer was satisfied with the quality and quantity of stores. In case of any objection the matter was to be reported to the Station Commander whose order on the subject would be final. This system of supplying rations to the Navy seemed very efficient but in practice it entirely depended on care and diligence of RIASC officers after they received consignments from the Food Department of the Government. Similarly such a role and procedure was followed when the

Base Victualling Office of the Navy received consignment for the Navy from RIASC. The negligence by any of these officers would determine the quality of ration supplies. There were numerous occasions when both of these officers would, in self defence, take self righteous positions whenever ration supplies were found below standard.

It was this basic and inherent deficiency in this supply procedure that did not let the quality of food improve in the Navy. Going by known facts, the bad quality of food was very well known to the Naval Authorities even before the 1946 mutiny. In June 1942 bad food was the main cause of mutiny by sailors on board HMIS *Konkan* at Tobermory UK. Their main complaint was regarding food. Firstly, it was the insufficient scale of rations for winter climate followed by bad quality of *atta* and bad cooking. There was a Board of Inquiry which found all these complaints to be true but 17 sailors were punished and dismissed from the Service. Even in May 1944 there were complaints of bad fresh ration supplies in MTE Bombay. Meat was reported to be bone only. Potatoes were bad, small and distasteful, cheap and stale seasonal vegetables and no other variety, no tomatoes or cauliflower was ever supplied. The dry rations were no better. Pulses (Dal) were only of two types and rice was with paddy and husk. These complaints were forwarded to the Flag Officer Commanding RIN.

Both the Army supply officers and naval victualling officers stood by their correct roles but the truth emerged in the letter of Quarter Master General of India dated 6 July 1944 to Headquarters Eastern Command. In this letter he mentioned that old stocks of RIASC supplies were issued to RIN against their demands for purpose of turn over. Many improvements were suggested but it was self admission that supplies to Navy were not up to standard. There were some more deliberations at higher levels after this letter but hardly any improvement noticed in the quality of rations supplied to the Navy. Again in April 1945, NHQs complained of bad quality of grain and grain products-atta supplied to RIN doubting whether the present arrangement of inspection of grains and grain products was effective. The War Department, in turn, informed this to the Food Department.

The quality of rice supplied to the Navy was also no better. In late 1945 there were complaints of bad rice from many naval establishments in Bombay. HMIS *Dalhousie* and HMIS *Talwar* reported that cooked rice bore offensive smell and a large quantity of stones. To get rid of smell, the washing of cooked rice was suggested by naval authorities, not knowing that washing of cooked rice would turn it into pulp and make it totally unfit for human consumption. This complaint was forwarded to Brigadier Nicol of the Food Inspection Wing of Quarter Master General of India. On 12 January 1946 he decreed that rice was of good quality but NHQs was not satisfied with this answer. The issue was then reported to the Administrative Officer on 21 January 1946. It stated that numerous and continued complaints were being received regarding bad quality of rice supplied to the Navy by RIASC. The investigations proved that the rice was dirty. It contained large percentage of empty husk, stones, foreign matter and was of offensive smell and bad taste after cooking. These complaints were causing great concern but this report also did not evoke any favourable response. Before taking up this complaint, NHQs had sent Lieutenant Colonel Haq Nawaz of Personnel Directorate at Delhi to visit Bombay. He not only found these complaints to be true but he also found a bundle of leaflets in the War Information Room of HMIS *Talwar*. The contents of the leaflets were:-

"AN EYE HERE ALSO. PLEASE VISIT GLORIOUS HELL IN BOMBAY –VERSOVA OUR DEMOB CENTRE - WITNESS THESE, OUR SUFFERINGS-HUNGER - INJUSTICE - OPPRESSIONS"

A very large number of establishments and sailors were located in Bombay area. The complaint of bad food was common in almost all establishments. The common general talk among them regarding service conditions and bad food helped spread discontent among men at Bombay. The complaints of bad service conditions were also heard at the Release Centre HMIS *Kakuari*. The men had rendered yeoman service during war and were now departing with unpleasant memories of naval service.

(e)   Other reasons

(i)   Personnel

Food was the main grouse resulting in the hunger strike of sailors. It brought about unity among the sailors of all branches and gave them cause to defy Service discipline. As a result there was a total breakdown of naval administration. Service discipline is a binding force between men and their officers. The three pillars of the Naval Service are (i) Officers and Men- especially officers, (ii) Proper Training – both Technical and Service discipline and (iii) Administration. Lack of training may result in inefficiency but faltering administration adversely affects the morale of men and lowers the respect and their bondage of discipline. Lack of discipline severely cripples the administration.

(ii)   Lack of training

The right type of men for the right job in the Service is axiomatic. The right instructors, training facilities and curriculum of instructions with systematic training are essential to develop personnel to be good officers or sailors after entry in the service. In naval training establishments it is the good instructor, officer or senior sailor, who had to set a good example, to train and bring trainees up to the mark. Any dereliction or bypassing this time tested method impedes development. Good basic training is the main naval foundation for technical training, inculcation of service discipline, team work and managerial skills especially for officers and senior sailors. The social and cultural background of trainees and men on board ships and establishment must also be kept in view for overall efficiency in any naval unit.

The sudden expansion of the Navy after the outbreak of World War II adversely affected the recruitment procedure and the training of personnel. There was acute shortage of regular naval officers. From 1940 a large number of Royal Indian Naval Reserve (RINR) and Royal Indian Naval Volunteer Reserve (RINVR) were recruited to add to regular service cadre officers. RINR officers were from the Merchant Navy. They were new to the Navy but had some sea experience. RINVR were direct recruits and had different backgrounds. Some were university educated Indians but the majority were Englishmen from British companies and Tea Gardens in India. They did not apply but being British subjects they were conscripted for service in the navy. The 'Reserve Officers' wore wavy pattern thinner lace stripes of gold on shoulder epaulettes whilst regular officers had straight broad gold lace stripes on their epaulettes. Their training was of 15 weeks duration as against roughly four years of training for direct entry officers. The professional training for these officers was in Seamanship, Signals-Communication, Navigation, Gunnery and Torpedo-Anti Submarine subjects. Each course was of 3 weeks duration. Training in all streams left much to be desired. The Gunnery School then was in a mansion on Malabar hill. It taught gunnery on an unusable 12 Pounder gun with a range of choicest abusive curses to British gunners in field training courses. Lectures on 'rules of the road' and self-study of seamanship volumes with a few visits to any ship in harbour would cover a complete course for seamanship. During war, a flotilla of motor launches was to be commissioned. Some 'Reserve' under training officers were pulled out from courses and sent to these crafts to keep it operational. Lack of training had neither honed professional skills nor infused leadership qualities in officers. The deficient leadership quality gave rise to unservice-like manners and bad attitudes of officers.

(iii)   Foul language

English was the working language between officers and ratings. For better communication, officers were encouraged to learn 'Roman Urdu' (Urdu in English script) and the ratings also had learnt to speak Pidgin English. This peculiar type of naval way of communication with a stock of foul vocabulary both in English and Urdu languages was known to be common practice and taken as normal without any malice. A British commander of a ship generally gave orders to the men in the wheel house of his ship by calling him *'ULLO, course pe jao'* but there was no mutiny on his ship. Gunnery branch used maximum lung power when conducting field training and gun drills. The trainees could hardly make out whether they were being taught or shouted upon. It seemed that all this was to personify the harshest arrogant face of an officer. It was common talk among men of those times that Lieutenant AK Chakravarty, (retired as Rear Admiral), the only Indian Officer in the Gunnery School at Karachi, was a terror for both the staff and the trainees. He and Commander King, who later was appointed commanding officer of HMIS *Talwar*, did a Long Gunnery Course together at HMS *Excellent* (Portsmouth). There might have been umpteen times of bad mouthing by any officer or senior sailor but the foul utterances of Commander King became the main cause to ignite mutiny in the Navy.

(iv)   Daily administration –A planned negligence

Basically naval administration is part of the chain of command and control. Naval Headquarters heads this administrative chain and Station or Command Headquarters are the highest naval authorities in their respective areas. All ships and naval establishments in their respective areas are headed by suitable officers designated as 'Commanding Officers' who is assisted by a second-in-command known as 'Executive Officer'. 'Departmental Officers' head their departments in that ship or establishment. In this chain of administration, the role of Commanding Officers, Executive Officers, Departmental Officers and Senior Sailors has always been considered as very important. Sailors of the same department are grouped together into 'Division' and looked after by officers of the same department known as their 'Divisional Officers'. Senior Sailors, known as Divisional Chief/Petty officers assist the Divisional officer. In practice they hold the key to high morale and good discipline in their men. It in no way meant to suggest that higher command is absolved of these responsibilities. It is always the higher command that alleviate the grievances/ difficulties brought to its notice through this chain of command better known as 'proper channels' by which the naval administration reaches out to the men in naval service. With the breakdown of the administration in HMIS *Talwar*, Bombay command was under severe strain. The recourse to hunger strike showed passive resistance and mounting defiance of naval authority. The mutiny was around the corner.

7

Prelude to Mutiny

Bombay - Epicentre

It was HMIS *Talwar*, a shore establishment at Bombay, which became the centre of the 1946 Naval Mutiny. The very mention of Bombay brings nostalgic memories of its great importance to India. Any ship under any flag which came to Bombay would have remembered it or would like to visit it gain. The conglomeration of seven tiny islands of Colaba, Fort, Byculla, Parel, Worli, Matunga and Mahim known as Bombay now extends to Mulund and Dahisar. It is no more an island now but a sort of peninsula. It is a historically important city and in varying fortunes it saw many ups and downs. In 1534 it was ceded to the king of Portugal by Sultan Bahadur shah, at a princely rent of 85 pounds sterling a year. An Anglo-Dutch fleet conquered/looted it and left. In 1661 Portugal gave it to the king of England as dowry, who in turn gave it to the East India Company in 1668. After the First War of Independence (Mutiny) in 1857 India had become a colony of the British Empire. In 1862 the old fortification was demolished and present day Bombay took shape. In 1869 after the opening of the Suez Canal, maritime trade boomed and Bombay rode the waves of prosperity and became famous-indeed a Gateway to India.

Bombay is not only the commercial hub of India but the birth place of the Indian National Congress also and closely linked to the Indian Political struggle. The demands for Swaraj (self-government), *Purna Swaraj* (Complete Independence) were announced from here. The 'Quit India' resolution was passed by the Congress Committee at the meeting at Gowalia Tank in Bombay on 8 August 1942. This was a mass movement and a clarion call for the Independence of India. Sailors are not politicians but like the Indian political struggle it was destined that their 1946 struggle for justice had also begun in this great city. Such is the charismatic greatness of Bombay. The sailors, coming from remote corners of India for service in the Navy, were stirred by the aura of Bombay and mettle of INA determination in order to be ready to defy British naval authorities. The 1946 mutiny was fast casting its shadows over all naval establishments in Bombay in the true spirit of this historic city.

The end of World War II and victory celebrations would have been the last joyous occasion for sailors but soon distrust and uncertainty raised their ugly head. The political atmosphere became surcharged with rumours that Britain was not inclined and in no hurry to free India and were furtively sowing the seeds of hatred. Almost everyone believed that freedom of India was not a possibility till the Labour Government was formed in England. These political uncertainties had confused both the rulers and the ruled. It may not be out of place to say that in such conditions of uncertainties agitating ratings may have looked up to political parties and interested parties would have made clandestine contacts with men in naval uniform to further their respective causes. Bad service conditions were a common grouse and a unifying factor for the sailors to get help for getting their complaints and grievances redressed. These exploits however per se, were considered achievable through clandestine contacts. Under these equally confusing and suspicious circumstances, the loyal and inactive ratings would have postured as the three proverbial monkeys of Gandhiji who saw nothing, heard nothing or said nothing. In such unconcerned surroundings, the fear of being reported or booked on the sly was considerably reduced. This in turn gives raw courage to any would be adventurer to indulge in unlawful activities with missionary zeal and confidence without assuming leadership. Such must have then been the state of affairs prevailing in HMIS *Talwar* when the bugle of mutiny was sounded in this establishment for the first time. It must have galvanized all who sympathized with the cause and put the fear of God in those who thought themselves invisible.

Navy Day at HMIS *Talwar*

RIN was a true replica of the Royal Navy except that all ratings were Indian. It followed all customs and traditions of the Royal Navy which also included anglicized behaviour of Indian officers which at times was more arrogant than their British counterparts. Seven folds on trousers and white stripes on blue collars of ceremonial uniforms of ratings depicted seven seas and victories of the British naval captain Nelson. Navy Day celebrations were the commemoration of British traditions which glorified the Royal Navy and its naval saga. The Royal Navy was traditionally the senior service in Britain. Its 'Navy Day' was a solemn occasion of pride. On Navy Day, all ships and Naval Establishments are decorated, in naval terminology called "Dress Ship", and ships are opened to the public. Navy Days always attracted sizeable crowds who visit naval Ships and Establishments. 'Navy Day' functions are attended by highest dignitaries of the country.

Traditionally, Navy Day was also celebrated by the Royal Indian Navy but the dates of Navy Day varied. In 1944 RIN celebrated Navy Day in the month of October, its commissioning month in 1934. In 1945, due to preoccupation with victory celebrations at the end of the war, Navy Day was decided to be celebrated on 1 December 1945. After victory in World War II the significance and importance of this Navy Day was far more significant. It was an occasion when the whole Navy would be in the lime light and all eyes would focus towards it. An untoward incident on this day would get widest publicity and create great embarrassment for the Royal Navy, the senior service of the British Crown, and helps strengthen and progress Indian Independence. It was the same national cause that the Congress by its non-violent movement and other political parties by their own programmes were planning against British rule. The only difference was that it was not a mass movement but a plan devised by the naval ratings for 'Navy Day' which was restricted and known only to few in HMIS *Talwar*. Incidentally the Indian Navy now celebrates Navy week during the first week of December every year to commemorate successful Naval Action in the 1971 War against Pakistan and had set its own tradition.

The Officers and ship's company of Talwar had put in hard work and spared no effort to make their establishment ship-shape for Navy Day celebrations. It was a known fact that this naval establishment was woefully overcrowded with sailors awaiting release from service. Most of them were frustrated due to deteriorating service conditions of service and shadows of an uncertain future staring them in their faces. They might not have been whole heartedly enthused by these celebrations but rigged up establishment for the Navy Day. Knowing the importance of these celebrations the Commanding Officer, Lieutenant Commander Coles, with high hopes, would have heaved a sigh of relief on completion of preparations for Navy Day. All would have wished it a great success.

On these high notes and high hopes, courtesy proverbial slip between the cup and lip, misfortune haunted this establishment. The serenity of the occasion, peace and quietness in the establishment resembled the lull before the sea storm. On the night between 30 November and 1 December 1945, during the middle watch (0000-0400 hrs), when the ship's company had gone to sleep and others closed up for duty, a group of dissatisfied ratings, hitherto unknown to naval authorities, hoisted brooms and buckets on the signal mast head. They silently and secretly painted the parade ground and walls with subversive slogans. Some of these slogans had political overtones, like, "Inqalab Zindabad", "Quit India" and anti-British slogans like, "Kill the white dogs", generally heard in political rallies. They had completed their task with great efficiency and soon they were back in their beds pretending to be sound asleep. Dawn broke the lull and soon telephones were buzzing and action to salvage the situation was underway right away. The administration was clueless and was completely taken by surprise. The first signal of coming up of mutiny flashed on the night of 1 December 1945.

Discreet investigations followed but none knew who the perpetrators of this subversive act were. The action taken by the Commanding Officer of *Talwar*, Lieutenant Commander Coles, was to obliterate the painted slogans and the other symbols of smacking insolence in his establishment as also simultaneously reporting the incident to higher Naval authority in Bombay. The news of slogan writing at *Talwar* would have also spread like wild fire through word of mouth with the Navy Day publicity. The enormity of this incident must have been a great anti-British media hype. On 1 December 1945 the Bombay Chronicle Newspaper published an equally adverse article about RIN on this Navy Day.

Extract from article published in the Bombay Chronicle on 1 December 1945

"ROYAL INDIAN NAVY Story of India's National Humiliation"

- By 'Politicos'

Today the RIN celebrates the 'Navy Day'. Parades will be held in important centres of the country to make the might of "SHOW NAVY". There may be speeches too, to announce to the credulous audience the good faith of the benign Government and the incompetence of India to defend herself. This Navy Day 'Tamasha' is the second of the series. Last year Admiral Godfrey selected 21 October to celebrate it. That date was chosen because it coincided with the victory of the Royal Navy at Trafalger in 1805. Slaves in everything, we have to be slaves in choosing dates too, not to celebrate an event to mark the achievement of the Indian Navy but to rejoice the victory of the Royal Navy. Gods at Delhi thought otherwise. October seems to have proved too hot so the celebration of was postponed to 1 December this year.

In the realm of Indianisation of officer ranks during the war large numbers of young men have volunteered. The number of officers in both the reserves and all branches of the service is about 2000 officers. These officers have been trained in India, and in majority of the cases they have been trained by Indian Instructors. They have manned successfully the ships of the Royal Indian Navy for the past six years and won praise from the most conservative brass hat.

In addition to the Indian nationals the Government has been so large hearted as to grant commission to a number of foreigners. These include 1 American. 9 Dutch, I French, I Turk, I Goan, 5 Iraqis, 3 Jews, 11 Norwegians, 2 Russians, 2 Swedish and I Yugoslav. Can you beat this? The RIN is really Indian because the Indian tax payers pay to keep the Navy. But it is hardly Indian in officers as only about 45% officers are Indian – and that too during the war.

The war is over now, and the problem of post-war Navy is uppermost in everyone's mind. The Government of India has announced the demobilization plan by which nearly 9000 men and officers will be demobilized by April 1946.

Insult to India and Indian Officers

This will be the first batch of releases. It has also been announced that the pre-war cadre of officers by 106 of which 66 will be Indians and remaining Europeans. One may naturally ask if this is so because the Government cannot find amongst the two thousand odd Indian officers even 106 officers who could man the Navy. This number is itself an insult to the country. For the size of India's coastline this number is not at all adequate. The Government has chosen to render India impotent to defend itself. Trained personnel are being demobilized because the Government has evidently no desire to build a Navy. To add insult to injury we have to accept 40 European officers, it seems that it is not enough for Britain that India should be rendered crippled. She wants to keep in Indian Services English officers as constant reminders of national humiliation. It is high time that the Government understood that the last commodity that the Indian wishes to import is the Englishman.

Demobilization Centre - Sea Of Discontentment

Bad conditions of naval service were indeed intolerable and the endurance of ratings had been stretched to its limit. The loss of job was a constant source of despair and non-payment of all dues on demobilization was sadistically inhumane. Not that the naval authorities were unaware of these feelings but naval administration had turned a 'Nelson eye' and seemingly were immune to the grievances of the sailors. It was the duty of the naval administration to look after their men and to send them to their homes satisfied and not grumbling against the naval service. All had served the Royal Indian Navy with loyalty during the war. Naval Authorities could easily find satisfactory solutions to their grievances but it paid no attention to their sufferings.

The callous and unsympathetic attitude of naval administration per force had to be tolerated and borne by the ratings. Their verbal and written complaints regarding service grievances and service matters were not only set aside but met with maltreatment and hounding by the Provost Branch. Some dissatisfied ratings resorted to anonymous letter writing to bring their plight to the notice of higher Naval Authorities. One such letter giving the true picture at HMIS *Kakuari*, 'the Release Centre of the Navy' at Bombay (Versova), was received at Naval Headquarters on 16 November 1945. It largely mentioned that "Sleeping and messing arrangements for thousands of ratings awaiting release are more dreadful than those endured during the Bengal Famine. One wonders whether if he was in an enemy concentration camp he would have received better treatment than now meted out at *Kakuari* and its responsible Authorities. The men are drafted to the general pool (COOLIE COMPANY) where all sort of dirty jobs, like stone breaking and road making were regularly done.

About the same time, another anonymous letter, purportedly written by Communication sailors released from *Kakuari*, was received by NHQs at Delhi. It read, "We were released from *Kakuari* a month ago but we are sorry to say that our pay accounts are not cleared, Nearly Rs 200 is due to each of us so we refused to sign the pay sheet. On the day when we were released an officer threatened us with punishment. We were never punished during the Service. At the last moment we did not want to be punished, therefore, we signed the pay sheet and were released from the Service."

The third anonymous letter written by HO (Hostilities Only) sailors from *Kakuari* was also received at NHQs in November 1945. It read, "Injustice is being done in the RIN when in the military every man is paid all his dues – gratuity with 56 days pay. RIN is keeping all the things pending. If a rating is demanding his dues he is taken to task. Especially Gul Zaman RPO is disgracing all. Is this a reward for our faithfulness? HO ratings offered their services not for the sake of money like other Short Service Reserves. The concessions of railway, payments are coming slowly but the men were packed through fast".

A poster recovered from *Kakuari* summed up the situation there as follows:-

"AN EYE HERE ALSO PLEASE VISIT THE MOST GLORIOUS HELL IN BOMBAY - VERSOVA -OUR DEMOB CENTRE

WITNESS HERE OUR COMPLAINTS - HUNGER – INJUSTICE HERE. OUR COMPLAINTS, HUNGER INJUSTICE OPPRESIONS WITNESS HERE BROOM and BUCKET PARADE AT 6:30 AM EVERY MORNING. IS THIS THE REWARD FOR OUR LOYALITY SERVICE DURING WAR."

The anonymous letters and posters might have exaggerated adverse service conditions and might have been categorized as misguided acts of disgruntled and frustrated ratings awaiting release from Service. Even the statement of sailors who signed on a blank payment form as advised to them by an officer on behalf of Commodore JW Jefford, Commanding RIN Depot (RIN Barracks) may be doubted as incorrect. All doubts were set aside when the Commanding Officer of HMIS *Kakuari*, Captain Learmont in his statement to the Board of Inquiry openly admitted that there were glaring administrative deficiencies in release procedures. This amply highlights the fact that release procedures caused greater confusion to men resulting in open controversies creating dissatisfaction against the Naval Service. Captain Learmont mentioned two cases brought to his notice by his staff.

(1) A stoker joined the service three years earlier as stoker class ii and rendered satisfactory service on board ship before he was sent for release from the Navy. He qualified in the stoker course for promotion to the next grade but neither professionally nor financially did he get any benefit of it. His career was seriously

affected for no fault of his. It was clearly the failure of the department and divisional system of RIN.

(2) A number of sailors who reported to the Demobilization Centre were not given any war leave for last 2 to 3 years owing to engagements in war operations. They were entitled to war leave yet it was neither given during the entitled year or before their release. Their leave could not be accumulated or encashed.

Such cases showed complete lack of concern by the Naval Administration regarding welfare of ratings coming to the Release Centre before leaving the navy. Not to speak of other such administrative lapses on account of delays due to incomplete 'Pay statements'. 'Kit Lists' etc. Captain Learmont was highly critical of some frivolous kit items of no further value after usage but were being compulsorily collected or money in its lieu being charged from the ratings before their release from the service.

The Board asked FOCRIN as to why such a condition of maladministration that spreads dissatisfaction in the service was allowed to develop in the RIN?

Vice Admiral Godfrey, FOCRIN lamented to the Inquiry Commission 'I think undoubtedly the end of war caught us unprepared. The war ended a year earlier than was expected. Everybody was in the same condition both in India and Great Britain". *{Same like the beginning of the war}*

Though ration scales slightly differed the same kind of rations were supplied to the Navy, Army and Air Force but it snowballed in acts of indiscipline in the Navy only. In case it had taken place in all three Defence Forces it would have certainly surpassed the 1857 uprising and possibly been much more challenging to the war exhausted British rule in India. Bad service conditions in the other two services were not allowed to develop in an uprising but in the Navy the Naval Authorities allowed the situation to drift to an open mutiny. Perhaps the Navy was small and easier to control than the Army and Air Force. Disabling RIN Ships with local British resources was far easier and did not involve any outsider. A quick surgical operation snuffed out naval mutiny and enforced unconditional surrender, adding a last glow to the fast declining 'British Glory' in India.

Britain had fought World War II with the help of Indian Forces yet they were found wanting in administration of Indian naval personnel in ensuing peace time. The Naval Authorities were aware of their administrative disabilities but preferred to ignore and let the state of affairs to drift and grow into a mutiny. The apathetic manner in which the senior most service had conducted itself is hard to reconcile. It is equally hard to understand Vice Admiral Godfrrey's (FOCRIN) statement made to the Board of Inquiry that the war ended a year earlier. It was an open admission by the senior most naval officer in India that Great Britain did not control the events of war and they were not masters any more. In 1942 Americans had come to India and the British government was providing facilities and services to them. It is best described by Commander King who was then Staff Officer at Naval HQs Delhi. Quote "The arrival of General Wingate and Colonel Fergusson in IDG (Indian Delhi Gymkhana) is worth mentioning. They were doing something aggressive in Burma- we didn't know and story of the Chindits came out a lot later. Also there were many Americans arriving and taking up jobs of one sort or another. Further evidence of the United States' activities was the constant stream of aircraft- mostly Mustangs- refuelling at Delhi Airport and moving on towards the East." The era of British supremacy had run out.

In military jargon the Royal Indian Navy was looked upon as a ceremonial service and the Army as fighting force. I first heard it in January 1948 when some seasoned army personnel were my co- passengers in the military compartment during a journey to Bombay after my enrolment in the Navy. A show down with the Army would have been more hurting to British pride (1857 memories) than the uprising by a mere handful of junior sailors of a ceremonial service.

Soon after the war, Britain decided to reduce the strength of the RIN to peace time sanctions. It was analogous to the sudden decision of expansion of the navy with the outbreak of World War II. The consequences of these hasty decisions were best known to the British authorities. The sudden expansion caused discontentment and sudden mass demobilization took the shape of the 1946 mutiny of sailors. Both these decisions were the prerogative of the British Government. But it is an interesting fact that when Britain was fast reducing its Indian naval strength to its peace time establishment, its Admiralty in London had already approved the induction of one Light Cruiser, HMIS *Achilles* to the Royal Indian Navy. The crew for this ship was undergoing training in UK much before the independence of India. On partition of India in August 1947 these naval personnel were asked the choice of opting for India or Pakistan. The sale of this ship, later renamed HMIS *Delhi*, was already in the pipe line before independence of India.

The appointment of Admiral Lord Mountbatten as Governor General of India helped RIN to remain in the lime light and expansion of the Navy continued under the new Commander In Chief of the Navy, Vice Admiral Edward Parry who succeeded Vice Admiral Godfrey. It is interesting to mention that the RIN was the senior most service and it received the President's Colours on 27 May 1951 from the first President of India Dr Rajendra Prasad before President's Colours were awarded to the Indian Army. After independence, Britain was the main supplier of naval hardware to both Indian and Pakistan Navies. The Royal Navy trained their personnel in Submarine and Naval Aviation branches though these Arms were introduced in Indian and Pakistan Navies at much later dates. Both countries, India and Pakistan, bought British obsolete and redundant war surplus equipment at substantial rates. The expenditure for training of a large number of naval personnel in England and the cost of acquisition of equipment from Britain considerably reduced British War debts to India and Pakistan. The British were undoubtedly clever diplomats and most efficient traders. They came to India in the guise of a trader, ruled India and finally departed from Indian soil trading their redundant and obsolete defence hardware to the now newly independent countries, India and Pakistan.

8

Escalation

Change of Commanding Officer

Bad service conditions had caused discontent and some miscreants had painted subversive slogans at HMIS *Talwar* on Navy Day. Nobody was caught indulging in this act. As a result, there was mistrust between the officers and naval ratings. The miscreants must have rejoiced at their success but the incident was like a bolt from the blue for the Commanding Officer. The loose talk in the mess decks would be making a mockery of the command and boosting the resolve of these miscreants for such actions in future.

The naval authorities were aware of unsatisfactory service conditions prevailing in some naval establishments in Bombay. Many anonymous letters voicing these had been received at the naval headquarters in Delhi. Subversive writing at *Talwar* on the night of the 'Navy Day' jolted and goaded the naval authority at Delhi for some action. It was under these circumstances that Lieutenant Colonel M Haque, Deputy Director, Morale and Security, at NHQs was sent to these naval units at Bombay. In those days, the morale and security of naval personnel at the naval headquarters was under the naval administration but looked after by the Army officers who also looked after other naval departments like logistic services such as Ordnance stores, Victuals and Medical stores. The navy just operated naval ships and imparted training in their respective professional training establishment and deployed the men under its command for professional duties afloat and ashore. In the directorate of personnel, functions like transfers, training and promotion were with naval officers but morale and security of these naval personnel was the responsibility of the army officers at naval headquarters. Lieutenant Colonel Haque was the Director, Morale and Security at NHQs and he visited these naval establishments at

Bombay. His report was not of much comfort to the authorities. An urgent administrative action was inevitable to control the deteriorating situation and so it was decided to change the Commanding Officer. Therefore Lieutenant Commander Coles, commanding *HMIS Talwar* was replaced with Commander AF King.

HMIS *Talwar* was a naval Signal-Communication Centre and School. As per the naval conventions, all training establishments and its subunits are normally commanded and staffed with officers and men from the same branch for better professional efficiency. Lieutenant Commander Cole was from the Communication Branch and Commander King belonged to the Gunnery Branch. Some basic professional characteristics help to encourage and cultivate professional affinity and efficiency. Their working conditions also differ very much. The communication sailors work in close proximity with their officers whilst the Gunnery officers are aloof from their men. Closeness develops working understanding in this department. Gunnery officers hold a distinct air of superiority whether they command parades or conduct gun drills which often convey an unambiguous sense of control over the men. It is likely that the nearness of Lieutenant Commander Coles, for professional reasons, was misunderstood. He was deemed to be pro-Indian and friendly to men under him in HMIS *Talwar*. Commander King was preferred for a wide and varied all around experience in naval service and duties at the naval headquarters. He was senior in rank to Lieutenant Commander Coles.

New Commanding Officer – Commander King

The new Commanding Officer Commander King was born on 2nd October 1917. Towards the end of 1934, at the age of seventeen years, he appeared in an examination for selection of cadets in the Royal Navy. Due to low marks in the French language paper, he was not selected for the Royal Navy but instead was trained as a cadet for service in the Royal Indian Navy. After training in United Kingdom he was sent to Bombay for service with RIN at the end of 1936. During the waiting period at Bombay, he was also available for outside duties and he was detailed to escort the then Governor of Bombay, Lord Brabourn on his boat journey to Elephanta. It was his first duty in India. When boarding Lord Brabourn enquired from the Barge–in–Charge about its location on the coast. King cut in saying "Don't worry, Coxswain knows it." The boat journey was a 45 minutes trip to Elephanta Island. Next day, the ADC to the Governor called for Boat

Officer King to meet the Governor. H.E asked him how long he had been in India. "Two days, Sir", was the prompt reply. Thereafter, the Governor gave him an interesting talk about the political situation at that time and how the 'Indianisation' of service had to take on new momentum. He could never forget this discussion although till that time he had not given even a single thought to this subject. At the outbreak of World War II, some Portuguese merchant ships were stranded at the Goa harbour. He was sent on an intelligence task of conveying instructions to the British Vice Consul there to keep an eye on these ships. In the early 1940, he underwent a Gunnery Course at *HMIS Excellent* in Portsmouth UK. During the training, he took part in a naval raid and seized two French Destroyers as these would be captured by the Germans after the surrender of France. Back in India he carried out duties of Gunnery Staff Specialist Officer at NHQs. He would accompany Admiral Fitzherbert and later Admiral Godfrey whenever inspection of any Gunnery site or Gunnery equipment was needed for use by RIN. He found Admiral Fitzherbert to be very pleasant and Admiral Godfrey of energetic and brilliant mind but of hot temper. They both assessed him with complimentary words like zealous, common sense, imagination, loyalty and tact in their annual reports. Politically, Commander King was conscious that the "Quit India" campaign was organized to disrupt the British administration, this civil disobedience movement was aimed at disruption of British War effort as also the implications of support for Indian National Army.

In 1944, King had attended the Tactical Anti-Submarine course at Liverpool. It concerned operation of German Submarines and U Boat warfare. Some intelligence reports indicated that the threat of enemy submarines was expected to extend to Eastern Seas also. He was engaged in setting up of these facilities at Bombay and scouting for recruiting suitable personnel for this task when the war ended. There was no other officer trained for these duties. He had organized A/S Tactical exercise which was attended by Vice Admiral Godfrey, FOCRIN and Rear Admiral Rattray Flag Officer, Bombay. After Deputy Director Morale and Security Director, Lieutenant Colonel Haque had submitted his report on the Navy Day incident at Bombay, Commander King was told to join them for a briefing by the Army Chief in their daily meetings. He was appointed as the Commanding Officer of HMIS *Talwar* and took over these duties from Lieutenant Commander Cole on 21 January 1946.

The change in command indicated an expression of unhappiness of senior naval authority with the previous Commanding Officer, Lieutenant Commander Coles for not any professional deficiency but due to the incident on the eve of Navy Day. It was mainly because of his inability to prevent it and not catch any culprits of this incident. The removal from command in this manner is viewed as a punishment as it affects all further promotion in the service and hurts the professional pride. The change in command was like a minor success for the miscreants as their incident had rattled naval authorities. The professional gloom in the unit was a shot in the arm for the scheming ringleaders to renew their action plan and further rattle the navy. Like the sacked Commanding Officer, the officers under him would also be at a low morale. This gulf between these officers and the new Commanding officer would be discreetly watched and exploited by the miscreants to their advantage. It was in these circumstances that before Commander King could adjust himself to the new surroundings the miscreants staged another subversive incident in *HMIS Talwar* on 1 February 1946.

Incident on 1 February 1946

Within a few days of taking over the command, the offhanded behaviour of Commander King towards his ship's company embroiled him in two separate cases regarding service matters with two sailors. On the heels of these cases, another bold slogan writing incident, similar to that which took place on Navy Day was waiting to be repeated on the night of 1-2 February 1946 also. These cases were:-

(1) Two sailors were brought before Commander King for being absent without leave. He neither asked them any question nor sought the opinion of their Divisional officer Lieutenant Meredith but very casually glanced through their service documents and curtly pronounced severe punishment. Divisional officers are like welfare officers for men in the naval administration. Commander King wanted to convey in no uncertain terms that he meant business. His openly hostile behaviour towards the sailors would have brought bitter comments in the mess decks and more dislike for the new Commanding Officer.

(2) The second case possibly was to rattle the new Commanding Officer. It was a normal request in proper service manner to see the Commanding Officer regarding a service matter. RK Singh, a

plucky sailor, requested Commander King for permission to resign from the Navy. He had chosen to poke fun at the naval procedure and deride his new Commanding Officer. He was due to be released from service in the normal course of time but he wanted to resign instead. As per rules, sailors are not allowed to tender their resignation but they can only request for their release from the service. These are administrative niceties to maintain discipline in the service. RK Singh was punished for this tomfoolery but the incident created further animosity between Commander King and the sailors that further led to the deepening of the gulf between them.

Such were the irritants and pinpricks which had sullied humane values and very soon it was an open secret that there was an element of distrust and hostility between them. The ratings, by and large, carried the impression that the new Commanding Officer was sent to gun them down while the new Commanding Officer thought that the sailors from the communication branch completely lacked discipline and needed firm handling. There was total lack of team spirit between the ratings and their Commanding Officer. This kind of situation existed in the establishment when slogans were again written on the walls of *Talwar* on the night of 1-2 February 1946 before the visit of FOCRIN to this establishment. The change-in-command of *HMIS Talwar* did not produce the desired result. Naval administration was aggressive and the ratings were becoming defiant. Apparently these incidents were stage-managed to trouble the naval administration.

On 2nd February 1946, FOCRIN was scheduled to visit *HMIS Talwar*. It was his first visit to this establishment after the incident of slogan writing on Navy Day (1 December 1945). All efforts were made to give a face lift to the establishment yet there was an air of suspicion and uncertainty. Commander King would certainly take all the precautions to prevent repetition of the Navy Day episode and the rebels were equally determined to make a mark. It was a cat and mouse game between them on that night. Under these conditions, the saluting dais from which FOCRIN was to take the salute for the guard of honour was found painted with slogans like 'Jai Hind and Quit India' and some slogans were also found written with paint on the walls of *HMIS Talwar*. At midnight, under the watchful eye of the duty staff officer at the Naval Signal Centre, a leading telegraphist, BC Dutt was found moving about in a suspicious manner. The duty officer saw his hands were slightly stained. Commander King was informed immediately and L Tel Dutt was arrested. His locker was searched and some incriminatory papers including a revolutionary subversive pamphlet, a personal diary of January 1946 along with a few letters to and from his friends and two books, "Speeches of Pandit Jawaharlal Nehru" and "The Communist answer to the Congress charges" were recovered from his locker. Incidentally till then, his record was excellent and his good behaviour could even be vouched for by his detractor, Commander King. Perhaps Dutt was led astray by some revolutionary organization.

Contents of the Diary

1 January 1946 – "Welcome New year. You are to change the mode of my life and you might shake the very foundations of our National Life".

3 January 1946 – Is about his financial condition, It reads "I myself have not got enough to pull through the whole month.

4 January 1946, -" Lieutenant Cooper asked me if I'd like to be drafted to a PG and of course, I replied in negative. Put request to see Commanding Officer for immediate release as some nice jobs are vacant but CIO, the rogue finished it. This is the reward for five years of loyal and gallant service - this imperialist Government gives.

8 January 1946 – "Get a report of the foolishness of our boys. Our boys, with the exception of one, are all hopeless.

10 January 1946 – "Things are taking a bit gloomy shape"

13 January 1946 – "Whoever knows me with the exception of our two say your young mind will change after you are released".

28 January 1946 – "Mind is wondering. There is nothing I can put my mind on. Find interest in nothing except politics and the future is so much doubtful that concentration on politics too sometimes seems impossible".

His diary was carefully perused by the Board of Inquiry. In their opinion his writing leaves no room for doubt that he was in touch with some outsider organization, the object of which was to undermine the loyalty of the Forces. There were also words like "Boss, HQ our whis cam'. 'Whis cam' was abbreviation of whispering campaign. One of the papers in his possession set out the necessity for revolution in the forces and concluded, "There are three ways of British administration over our country – the ICS, the Police and the Forces. The Forces are the main weapon for maintaining their evil eyes in this holy land."

Text of the Pamphlets

The text of a pamphlet found in his locker reads:-

"For over 25 years now we have been actively trying to get rid of our British rulers but failed. Large sections amongst the Congress as also in the country (mostly vested interests) feel that we are not strong enough to fight the British and must therefore, try to win independence gradually through peaceful and constitutional methods. At Shimla, the Congress showed how anxious it was to come to a compromise with the Government at practically any cost.

Even when the Congress has fought the British in the past, the fight has mostly been precipitated by the British and also the terms have always been dictated by them.

The fight itself has been sporadic and aimed at the vaguer things called "British Imperialism" or some partial aspect of it like the 'Salt Act' or foreign cloth. Also it has been fought by a small section of our people who belong to the Congress or are closely affiliated to it.

The agents of the British Imperialism have never been touched by these struggles, nor have the non-Congress population at large participated in the fight, mainly because of Congress policy of isolation.

The result is that in spite of 25 years of struggle and bitterness, the Englishmen and their Indian servants are the most comfortable people in the country. The ranks of Government have never once threatened disruption and the agents of imperialism have never been personally made to feel unwanted. "God save the King" is played in all the public places and Indians stand at attention to it. The Union Jack flies whenever and wherever it pleases, even on the municipal buildings which house the Congress majorities.

This could not be so except with the consent, goodwill and cooperation of the Indians themselves. This means that the general will to get rid of the foreigner is non-existent in our country.

This also shows that slavery has become such a habit with us that we complacently accept not only the Englishman but also his flag and anthem and all that he stands for-viz, our exploitation, our slavery, our humiliation and often our death. In Bengal, millions died of starvation within the sight of food but not one dared to take it or fight for it – they begged for it and not receiving it, they just died.

As it should be, every Indian should be so conscious of his rights to freedom and to his country as to insist that every agent and emblem of our slavery must quit right here and now.

This stand is necessary not only to broad base our fight to include each and every Indian but is imperative for our ownself – respect and national character and integrity. It is downright shameful that a handful of foreigners can hold their own and be so comfortable in a country of four hundred million people who should on all account be uncompromisingly hostile – all the time, everyday must become 9 August, 1942 till freedom is won.

An Indian who does not resist the British in every way possible is a coward with no justification. There are no short cuts to freedom.

The British cannot do without India. It is either her suicide or ours. We have to, therefore, and must forcibly snatch our freedom from our rulers. The best way to do it is the WILL TO BE FREE. If every Indian wills to be free he must act as free. If he acts as free, he is free. No power on earth can dominate four hundred million against their will.

To infuse the will to be free which must mean a total boycott of and resistance to the Englishman. It is necessary to organize a trained cadre of true patriots, drawn mainly from demobilized ranks of our fighting forces, who will spread this message of freedom and resistance in the entire country. This cadre will not constitute a political party but its members will infiltrate into all the existing organizations and strata of society including the Government ranks, and carry on their work.

They will not oppose or discredit the Congress or any other national organization nor set up rival organizations. They will merely seek to supplement our national movement and struggle by organized propaganda and constructive work amongst the masses. Their objective will be supplementation, not sup plantation. Their work will be constructive and not destructive.

The only political theory this cadre will recognize is INDIA'S IMMEDIATE AND COMPLETE INDEPENDENCE.

The only political principle creed this cadre will subscribe to is the Congress stand of "August 42 of QUIT INDIA".

The only political principle this cadre will act upon is: GET THE JOB DONE".

The program of this cadre will be a complete boycott of everything British, including the men. This cadre will be known as 'AZAD HINDUSTAN.'

Members of this cadre will be known as "Azad Hindi.' The pledge each member will subscribe to is:-

'I DECLARE I AM AZAD HINDI. I SWEAR LOYALTY TO AZAD HINDUSTAN AT ALL COST, EVEN UNTO DEATH'.

'TO BE AZAD HINDI IS NOT POLITICS, NOR IS THE CONCERN OF MY RELIGION. IT IS MY INALLIENABLE BIRTHRIGHT WHICH NO POWER CAN DENY AND NO LAW FORBID.'

I BELIEVE THAT IF I WILL TO BE FREE, I MUST ACT AS FREE AS I AM FREE.

FROM THIS DAY ON I SWEAR I WILL ACT AS FREE AS TO THE BEST OF MY CAPACITY."

Dutt may have the will to achieve the goals set out in this pamphlet, but it is highly unlikely that he would have drafted or wrote it all by himself. In the mess decks or overcrowded living barracks/blocks, it would be well nigh impossible to conceal this sort of activity. The pamphlet found in his locker is most likely to be the handiwork of a propagandist of a radical extremist political party.

As per evidence of Rear Admiral Rattray Flag Officer Bombay, Dutt was friendly with another rating Deb, who seemed to have greatly influenced him and was released from the service in the 3rd week of January 1946. L Tel Dutt, in his letter dated 2nd February 1946, addressed to Deb, writes, "I am alright and all out in our great task but it seems that the boys are losing interest......As I have told you before and it still holds good, that is, they don't understand a bit that goes on around them. They are born as kids and will stick to the same originality......I knew the very first day that life will not be a bed of roses if I step on this road. So I am not losing my wits so soon and never will." Incidentally, Dutt was on the lookout for a job and applied for commission in the navy.

It was a singular triumph for the watchful administration under Commander King to have caught L Tel Dutt in the midst of a subversive act which he could not deny. They had reasons to be jubilant for the nice work done by them, but the arrest of Dutt did not put an end to slogan writing in *Talwar*. Their jubilation was very short lived. Subversive slogans were again found written in *Talwar* on the night of 6-7 February 1945. This time, the miscreants directed their anger against Commander King, their Commanding officer. 'QUIT INDIA' was written on his car and the car tyres were found deflated. He also received anonymous threatening letters. These were serious acts of indiscipline and warning signs of further decline in the naval discipline in *HMIS Talwar*. The postures by both, the Commanding officer and the miscreants, had hardened. Morale and discipline were at their lowest ebb and indiscipline could spin out of control in the establishment.

Explosive Portent

Morale and security reports were discussed and Commander King was duly briefed at GHQ before he took over command of *HMIS Talwar*. He followed the guidelines as briefed and these did not include any action to improve the service conditions that were agitating the minds of ratings in his unit. Obviously, the naval administration was not in favour of any improvement in the service. It was seriously bent on dealing with disciplinary problems with an iron hand and the ratings did not relent. In this battle of wits, though Commander King achieved a spectacular success in catching the culprit for writing slogans in *Talwar* within a short time of his arrival on 1-2 February 1946 but soon after, he had to face an another equally challenging incident on the night of 6-7 February 1946. One thing for sure, he suffered a setback to his self-esteem and was keen to reassert himself with a renewed vigour. Ever vigilant was the watchword to catch the culprits. All the officers and senior sailors were instructed accordingly, including reporting on any suspicious characters under them. All were to carry out surprise rounds during the day and in messes and barracks at odd times during the night. Men who indulged in subversive activities were well aware of these methods and contrived other methods to confront the administration. It was under these circumstances that on the morning of 8 February 1946, Commander King was taking surprise rounds in *Talwar* when some off duty communication ratings in the barrack were said to have made cat calls at the passer by WRINs (Women Royal Indian Navy) as he entered their barrack. Commander King allegedly used abusive language against these ratings. Later, he rang up Lieutenant Commander Shaw, his Second-in-Command, and told him about this incident. He told him that he was not satisfied by the behaviour of these RCO/CCO ratings and their routine. Lieutenant Commander Shaw informed the ratings of the Commanding Officer's displeasure with them. He thereafter, began calling these ratings turn by turn to further inquire into the matter. During his investigation, the ratings alleged that Commander King addressed them as 'Sons of bitches', 'Junglees 'and 'Coolies'. Thereafter at about 1240 hours Lieutenant Commander Shaw went to the office of Commander King to inform him about the result of his inquiry. During that time, Lieutenant Nanda (Later he became Chief of Naval Staff in the Indian Navy) and Lieutenant Ashirvadam, the Divisional Officer of these sailors were also present in the office of Commander King.

The next day, Saturday 9th February 1946, these 14 ratings put in a request and complained against the bad language used by Commander King to the second-in-command Lieutenant Commander Shaw, as per the normal service procedure. He interviewed majority of these ratings on Saturday and the others who were on duty were seen by him on Sunday, the 10th February. Realizing the serious implications of their complaints involving the Commanding Officer and the urgency of action to resolve the issue, he forwarded their requests to Commander King by Sunday noon for further action. This serious matter was explained in the accompanying note and later a copy of the same note was also given to Chief of Staff in the Navy office. The matter was now known to the Bombay command as well. Commander King did not attach any importance or even read this note. In the most indifferent and capricious manner, he decided to deal with the case as per normal laid out routine for 'Request men and Defaulters'. As per normal routine the 'Request men and Defaulters' are only taken up once a week on every Saturday. 'Request men and Defaulters' is a naval unit court of justice held by the Second-in-Command Executive Officer twice a week and once a week by the Commanding Officer to dispense justice to men under them by granting their legitimate requests and awarding punishment to the defaulting personnel. The urgency and the importance of this request of sailors were deliberately ignored to impress upon them that he was in no way disturbed by them. In such tense circumstances, he would like his orders to be carried out. This on-going conflict, the burning issue, well-known to both to Commander King and the Bombay Naval Command was put off till 16 February 1946, the next Saturday. The command took no action or showed no urgency to resolve this impasse. It solely depended on Commander King and consequently the ratings had to suffer the agony of the haughty and egotistical attitude of their Commanding Officer who supposedly was also to deliver justice to them. The cause of ratings was being deliberately ignored and this further lowered their confidence in their Commanding Officer, whilst the mute inaction of the Bombay Naval Command wished this ugly situation to sort itself out.

Most of the sailors felt that postponing this serious matter by naval officers was solely to suppress them by exerting fear of their rank and authority. This lack of trust in the administration further hardened into 'no trust.' Consequently, there was a visible breakdown of administration. Even the divisional officers of the sailors found it hard and cumbersome to strike any rapport with them. During the lull period, 9 -16 February 1946, discontent and mistrust against the commanding officer must have grown and simmered amongst personnel in other naval units also. It must have suffered another setback when on 16 February 1946, the day of his requests man, the commanding officer further extended this period by 24 hours to let the ratings reconsider and submit their requests with complete details of their complaints in writing. He warned them of consequences for failure to prove their allegations in their complaints. These ratings were again brought up to the commanding officer on 18 February 1946. They submitted their complaints as directed. The accused ratings and their equally accused Commanding Officer, acting as judge, were facing each other in the local naval court. This process of justice was completely unjustifiable as the accused and the judge was the same person. Their commanding officer was such a judge who also was an accused in his own court. The sailors stood their ground. The truth was buried deep in both of them as the mutiny started on this day.

There seemed to be no impartial witness to the occurrence between Commander King and the ratings. In their statement to the BOE of *Talwar*, the ratings struck to their version and Commander King said, "I walked into the barrack to reprimand the ratings and none took any note of me. I said, in a loud voice "STAND UP". I cannot remember word by word of what I said except that the ratings were reprimanded in the normal naval fashion in accordance with my report." What is 'reprimanding a rating in normal naval fashion' was not explained.

Lieutenant Commander Shaw's statement to the *Talwar*'s BOE about his 1240hrs meeting with Commander King where Lieutenant Nanda and

Ashirvadam were also present is, "When King was referring to the ratings in *Talwar* who had not stood up on his visit to their barrack that morning, he had used the expression 'Sons of Bitches and beggars.'"

As regards Lieutenant Nanda, the commission described his attitude in the witness box to be rather partial to Commander King. He agreed to the extent that Commander King in his meeting with Lieutenant Commander Shaw had used the words 'Beggars' with reference to the ratings. In the BOE of *Talwar* Lieutenant Nanda stated "I have had a lot of contact with Commander King and I have heard him very often using bad language which comes to him unintentionally".

Lieutenant Kohli who later became Chief of Naval Staff also gave evidence to the BOE of *Talwar*. He stated that when he met Commander King on 8 February 1946, the exact words that he used were 'Not a son of a bitch took any note of me'. He also stated "It appears that the language must have been used for 14 ratings to lodge a complaint at once. It is certainly my impression that Commander King was not used to dealing with communication ratings, especially the large number we had here and used the same treatment he accorded to the seamen ratings".

Lieutenant Ashirvadam was also supportive of the evidence that he heard from the ratings. The commission stated in its report that giving due consideration to the entire evidence they had heard and pursued together with the attendant circumstances and extracts from the BOE of *Talwar*, it was difficult to unbelieve the ratings version concerning the language used by Commander King. The ratings, 14 in number, (4 Christians, 7 Hindu and 3 Mohammadan) have no common apparent motive to join against their Commanding Officer. The Commission is of the view that, in their judgment, the abusive language imputed to Commander King was in fact used by him.

The chain of events leading to the outbreak of mutiny in *HMIS Talwar* was investigated by the Board of Inquiry. It did not inquire into the reason as to why Flag Officer Bombay failed to take note of the report submitted by Lieutenant Commander Shaw, the investigation officer and second-in-command of *Talwar* to his Chief of Staff, orally and in writing on 10-11 February 1946 regarding the case between the 14 sailors and Commander King. It is very likely that this report was also similar to the one given to the Board of Inquiry in *Talwar* which read "When King was referring to ratings in *Talwar* who had not stood up when he went to their barrack that morning he had used the expression 'Sons of Bitches and beggars''. Perhaps silence was a better option for Flag Officer Bombay because it was only very recently (21 January 1946) that Commander King was appointed the commanding officer of this troublesome establishment after due briefing at the GHQ.

The reason for the Flag Officer of Bombay not taking any note of the report by Lieutenant Commander Shaw indicated lack of propriety in the naval service. The Royal Indian Navy was under the Government of India and headed by the Flag Officer Commanding, Admiral J N Godfrey, R N Retired. Orders to RIN were issued by the Commander-in-Chief India, HE General Auchinleck. Like the other Principal Staff Officers (PSO), the Flag Officer commanding the Royal Indian Navy (FOCRIN) was also equated with the PSOs. The Navy was like a utility service and manned by the naval personnel for duties in naval ships and establishments. The efficiency of the naval service depended on the naval personnel but their morale and security was the responsibility of Army Officers. The navy was nominally a senior service and the Flag Officer commanding RIN was appointed with the concurrence of the Commander-in-Chief of India. Within a month of naval mutiny, Admiral Godfrey was replaced by Vice Admiral Patterson on 26 March 1946. The appointment of Admiral Patterson was concurred by the GHQ.

9

Recipe of Mutiny

Within a short period of time, *HMIS Talwar* became the hallmark of indiscipline in the navy. During the war, these ratings may have passed through very hard times but now they were part of a victorious navy and the majority wished for better treatment from the naval service. Political parties were pitching hard for independence and the INA trials rekindled this spirit. The over-ambitious naval personnel who had dabbled and hobnobbed with the political elements had been identified. Further deterioration in naval discipline could have been possibly arrested, had the naval administration given some indication of improvement in service conditions and favourably considered payment of all dues to the personnel awaiting release from the service. The chain of events shaping the confrontation between naval administration and the ratings reached an impasse when initially the 9 February, the case of 14 sailors against Commander King was first delayed by a week till 16 February and again postponed to Monday, the 18 February 1946. The fast declining morale of ratings could have been appropriately reversed but the administration allowed ratings to simmer in their smouldering discontent over the weekend. And it was very late, because the incidents of bad food on Sunday and an equally callous-cum-indifferent attitude of duty officers made the quiescent ratings to go on the course of mass disobedience and hunger strike against the administration, the path to mutiny.

Recipe of Mutiny - Bad Food

The menu of the food prepared and served in sailor messes of those times were very unique. There was literally no difference between 'Standard' (Non Vegetarian) and 'V' (Vegetarian) rations except for milk in lieu of mutton. Vegetables and pulses were same for both and these were cooked in a common kitchen but served separately on the respective counters. The breakfast invariably was always 'bread and dal'. Varieties of dal, be it 'channa', 'urd', 'tooer' or any other kind, continued to be served unchanged for a number of days. For eating with rice at lunch, the same dal was diluted and served as 'Patli Dal' to wet the rice. This type of messing for sailors was also experienced by the author after he joined RIN in January 1948.

The problem arising from bad messing started at supper time on the evening of 17 February 1946 when 29 ratings in two vegetarian messes refused to take their meals. They complained to the Duty Officer that they were served with an obnoxious type of mixture of dal and vegetable as meals for supper. Lieutenants Batra and Sachdeva were the Duty Officers. As per the statements of the witnesses, these officers neither informed the Commanding Officer nor took any effective steps to address their problem. They suggested tinned food for the ratings and also said that they were ready to permit ratings to go ashore on liberty to buy food from outside. Neither was food prepared nor did the ratings go ashore to buy food and they slept without food. It may be interesting to know that this type of food complaints were normal and not new or unknown to most officers of *Talwar*. The Welfare Officer, Lieutenant Commander Arlaud described this state of food problem in these words to the Board of Inquiry of *HMIS Talwar*, "Complaints about food have been numerous not with regard to the quality of food but the way in which it is prepared. On the day of the mutiny, they only complained about the food especially dal which was not fit for human consumption and it was what they gave to their horses in their own homes."

Monday, the 18 February 1946 was an ominous day for *Talwar*. The 14 ratings who complained about abusive language of Commander King were to be brought up before him. As luck would have it, the dal served for breakfast on this day was also not palatable. Therefore, a large number of ratings refused to eat breakfast and walked out of the mess deck shouting slogans. For the 8.45 assembly when the call for 'Fall-in' for the morning Divisions was sounded, no rating turned up at the parade ground. It was the first indication of the defiant behaviour of the ratings in *Talwar*. Commander King, the Commanding Officer came to the establishment at 9.15, sensed the situation and soon after left to home for breakfast without issuing any instruction to anyone. He came, he saw and left for home. By the time he returned after breakfast, the feelings had run high and 'JAI HIND' and such slogans were being shouted by the sailors. The ratings now formed small groups and indulged in heated discussions among themselves. The officers, who tried to call, contact or talk to the ratings to pacify them were booed and shouted down. This situation took a turn for worse when men on duty in the signal centre came and also joined them after their duty. The spark of mutiny had been ignited.

Signs of Mutiny

By all accounts it was becoming increasingly clear that the situation at *Talwar* was taking a turn for the worse from the morning of 18 February 1946. Commander King had come to *Talwar* and must have noticed that no rating was around the parade ground before forming the morning 'Divisions'. It did not strike any bell to him and without a word with any officer he went back home for breakfast. Lieutenant Commander Lisle Taylor rang him up to inform him that the ratings did not come for Divisions. The call was taken by Mrs King as by then the Commanding Officer had already left for *Talwar* after breakfast. After he came, he took stock of situation himself and later held a conference with the officers at 10.15 am in his office. He was amidst all controversies but kept aloof and isolated from the results of his own actions. When questioned by the Board of Inquiry about this morning conference, Commander King stated that he had forgotten the details of this conference held with his officers but started explaining disobedience and defiance by the ratings.

It was very likely that with initial success in getting the subversive element caught, Commander King had highly impressed Flag Officer Bombay Rear Admiral Rattray and the Navy Office. His reputation would have been fairly high with implicit faith in his ability to tackle newly developing unrest in the ratings of *Talwar*. This faith was so strong that Flag Officer Bombay ignored the report of unrest in *Talwar* brought to him by Lieutenant Commander Shaw for the first time on 18 February 1946. In his statement to the BOE conducted in *Talwar*, Shaw said, "I went to the Vithal House (housing Navy Office) at about 11.25 (18 February 1946) and met Admiral Rattray who was coming down the stairs with his Flag Lieutenant. I asked him what I should say to the watch who were on duty and were not relieved. His words as closely as I could remember then were "Well you must tell the truth and tell them what has happened." I replied, "Tell them Sir that *Talwar* has mutinied?" To which the Admiral said "Good God, no Shaw. What an awful thing to suggest. Tell them that they have refused duty." Mutiny was now taking place and known to Flag Officer Bombay.

When in KAKUARI, the Sailors Release Center, a similar situation had developed and it was on the verge of mutiny. It must be said to the credit of Captain Learmont, its Commanding Officer, who told the striking sailors that their grievances will be forwarded to Navy Office and in doing so he was able to pacify successfully his ratings by such an assurance but it never came from Cdr King. Even as late as this, the disobedience of ratings was amenable to pacification.

10

Course of Mutiny

The clouds of unrest of men were visible since the last Navy Day. Subversive slogans were written on the walls of HMIS *Talwar* and some subversive activities had also come to notice. The relation between officers and the ratings smelt suspicion and mistrust. It was not unusual to hear the complaints of bad food but it was mainly the illogical and irrational decisions of the Duty Officers when they dealt with complaint of bad quality of rations and bad cooking on the evening of 17 and morning of 18 February 1946. Their indifferent attitude surcharged an already vitiated atmosphere due to the arrogant attitude of Commander King to wards 14 ratings who had complained against him using abusive language. At such a tense time, due care and caution should have been exercised not to further stir up the pent up feelings of the ratings. The inconsiderate and confused administration with no guidance from Flag Officer Bombay added more grit and resolve to the attitude of the defiant ratings. The defiance of ratings in *Talwar* was moving towards mutiny hitherto unparalleled in the history of the Royal Indian Navy. Within a very short time, it had spread to almost all ships and establishments of the Navy and joined by sailors of all branches and all communities, Hindus, Muslims, Sikhs and Christians. They came from different parts of India, spoke different languages and may have held different political opinions, yet they joined together against the British Officers. They did not seek any guidance from any one. Senior sailors, being worldly wise, had kept aloof. Mistrust was such that senior sailors were also not asked by the officers to pacify disgruntled junior sailors. The ship's company of HMIS *Talwar* now visibly stood divided in three groups, junior sailors with simmering discontentment, isolated senior sailors and the officers, led by Commander King incensed to teach a lesson to defiant sailors.

Half hearted and late attempts by senior sailors (Chiefs and Petty Officers) and Divisional Officers failed to persuade ratings to join duty. With passage of time, confusion and disorder was turning from bad to worse and a show down seemed imminent. With complete breakdown of local command and control it was now left for Flag Officer Bombay to tide over this ugly situation. He came to *Talwar* at 1200 and tried to address the ship's company. The ratings were in no mood to listen to the Flag Officer. There was complete chaos and no semblance of orderliness in the meeting addressed by Flag Officer Bombay (FOB). It was so disorderly, that the Flag Officer Bombay could only manage to say, **"They should return to their duty before their grievances can be heard"** This was not sufficient to pacify the ratings. Events at *Talwar* were fast becoming chaotic and anarchic.

18 February 1946, HMIS *Talwar*, Bombay

0730 hrs - Hands to Breakfast was piped. Only ratings of Command Communication Office (CCO), who were to close up for watch at 0830 hrs, came for breakfast. The rest left the mess shouting slogans.

0905 hrs - Commander King arrived and left without giving any instructions to any one.

0945 hrs - Commander King returned when Division were piped and the men were to fall in for parade before going for work. No ratings other than CPOs. POs Instructors, RN ratings and WRINs (Women Royal Indian Navy) came to the parade ground. No junior sailor came for parade.

1045 hrs - After a conference with his officers the unruly situation at *Talwar* was reported to the Flag Officer Bombay by Commander King. As a precaution all WRINs were ordered to leave *Talwar*.

1130 hrs - All small arms and ammunition from the magazine was removed to Castle Barracks. FOB had not anticipated that the mutiny would spread to Castle Barracks also.

1200 hrs - FOB arrived and tried to speak to ratings. He told them before Inquiry could be made into their grievances they must return to duty. He left at 1220 hrs.

1700 hrs - FOB again addressed ratings and told them that Captain Inigo Jones had taken over command from Commander King. He instructed the ratings to appoint their representatives who should get themselves prepared with their list of grievances by 0930 hrs on 19 February 1946. He also impressed on them to return to duty unconditionally. He gave them assurances that their representatives would not be victimized. *(The cause of inciting sailors to become indisciplined was removed but no action was taken to remove the cause of their grievances)*

The ratings living in *Talwar* were employed for duty at **Central Communication Office (CCO)** and they did not go for duty. *Talwar* was always in touch with **Receiving Station at Colaba** through Duty Communication Staff. The news of 'Strike in *Talwar*' had reached Colaba. The ratings in Receiving Station Colaba also did not take food in the evening. By now about 2000 ratings had struck work. The ratings at W/T Station Mahul, another communication establishment, were working normally because the telephone lines to **W/T Station at Mahul** were broken but news of the strike in *Talwar* was spreading very fast. At about 2pm there was a rumour that communication sailors doing duty at **Dock Yard Signal Station** would go on strike. The next duty watch communication ratings who were to close up on duty at 4pm watch refused and did not report for duty. Officer-in-Charge of Signal Station decided to remove some of the equipment and abandon Dock Yard Signal Station. At 7pm Royal Naval ratings closed up in place of Indian Ratings and manned the signal tower in CCO. Virtually all the communication branch ratings in and around south Bombay were now on strike.

HMIS *Talwar* was in a very chaotic condition. The ratings that normally followed service discipline to perform their duty under guidance of their seniors were a confused lot. They were without guidance and did not know what and how to respond to the proposal made by FOB during his last visit wherein he asked them to appoint representatives and list their grievances. It was utter confusion as even the sailors who posed as their spokesmen were in two minds and did not have the nerve to shoulder this responsibility. They, as usual in chaotic conditions, were loudly boasting of their actions but not willing to take any responsibility. There were all sorts of arguments and suggestions but no firm proposal from any of the confused groups of the ratings. The senior sailors had kept themselves totally aloof from this messy situation. It was under such confused circumstances that a sizeable group of ratings assembled for electing their representatives as asked for by FOB. Leading signalman Khan was elected President and in all 14 members were elected members of the Strike Committee. They hurriedly finalized the charter of their demands for presenting it to the Flag Officer

Bombay. Khan was not any loud mouth leader but earlier when serving in HMIS *Khatiawar* he had then complained about bad victuals and food and that also had not produced any result. He was mild mannered and widely acceptable to the assembled men. L Tel BC Dutt who was earlier caught for subversive activities in *Talwar* also attended this meeting. His case, by then, had been forwarded to higher naval authority and was awaiting further orders. He had been released from closed custody. He was not member of the Strike Committee but he along with another sailor went to the office of FREE PRESS JOURNAL and conveyed the news of the strike by the ratings to the Press. The unrest and defiance of sailors in *Talwar* had gained more momentum and it was an open secret. It was just an uneasy calm before the storm of Mutiny spread to most of the ships and establishments of the Royal Indian Navy. The news of the impending visit of FOB to HMIS *Talwar* was also known in various naval establishments in Bombay and all awaited the result of this meeting.

19 February 1946

No untoward incident occurred in the intervening night. In the morning, a group of ratings in RIN transport armed with hockey sticks, clubs etc drove around Bombay committing acts of hooliganism. At 0930 FOB arrived in *Talwar* and a meeting was held with the representatives of the ratings. Some unruly parties of sailors from other establishments in Bombay had begun to arrive and the meeting with FOB was constantly interrupted. The demands put forward by the 14 representatives of the sailors were:-

(a) **No victimization of strikers.**

(b) **Immediate release of Tel RK Singh from Arthur Road prison. He wanted to resign from the Navy.**

(c) **Speedy demobilization in accordance with age and service group with reasonable chance of peace time employment.**

(d) **Immediate action against Commander King for inhuman behaviour and using foul language.**

(e) **Best quality of rations and Indian food.**

(f) **RN scale of pay, family allowance, traveling facilities and use of NAAFI stores.**

(g) **No kit return at time of release.**

(h) Immediate grant of more gratuity and treasury pay to men on release from the Service.

(i) Good behaviour of officers towards lower deck personnel.

(j) Quick and regular promotion of lower deck personnel to officers. Entry of officers from abroad to be stopped.

(k) A new Commanding Officer of Signal School to be appointed.

All above demands were requested to be decided by naval authorities and a national leader by 1700. The national leader was to be nominated by the Committee of Sailors.

The Sailors Committee had also lodged the following protests and these were also required to be registered with the Government of India:-

(1) Immediate release of Political Leaders as well as all personnel of Indian National Army including Captain Rashid.

(2) Immediate and impartial Inquiry into firing on the public all over India.

(3) Immediate withdrawal of Indian troops from Indonesia and the Middle East.

It is noteworthy that the demands by the 'Strike Committee' not only pertained to service condition and welfare of Sailors but also included complaints of political malaise. The account of what happened in *Talwar* was well known and widely circulating in Bombay. There was considerable sympathy and support for the cause of sailors and the demands put by them. At about 0930hrs approximately 2000hrs ratings from various other ships and establishments had come to the dockyard and assembled at Break Water. They staged a 'Sit down Strike.' The mutiny had now overtaken Bombay naval harbour. The 'Union Jack' had been hauled down from the mast heads of all ships and establishments and flags of 'Congress' and 'Muslim League' were hoisted instead. A large crowd of ratings had gathered in the harbour area. A meeting was also held in the 'Azad Maidan' by defiant sailors and they marched in procession shouting anti British slogans. They raised slogans like, 'Release INA and Political Prisoners', 'Withdraw Indian Army from Indonesia' etc. The ratings wore normal white working uniform but did not wear uniform caps. Some of these defiant ratings asked people to remove English hats. They indulged in this type of rowdy behaviour but by far they remained non-violent. The news of the naval strike in Bombay was broadcast on All India Radio and also published in leading newspapers. The strike by the sailors in Bombay was now known to all naval stations in Calcutta, Karachi, Vizagpatnam and Madras. The whisper of sympathy strikes taking place in these stations also started coming in from other naval stations. (See Annexure I)

The surging crowds of public and discontented ratings were on the roads demanding justice for the naval ratings. The Naval administration was no longer in command. Feverish deployment of Army troops was already under way and they were taking positions at all naval establishments whilst all safety measures were being ensured in all armouries and the ships in harbour.

Bombay Nerve Centre

Castle Barracks

The spark of the mutiny had ignited at HMIS *Talwar* but it was the Royal Indian Naval Depot, some distance away, (now called Castle Barracks) that was the nerve centre and hub of all activities. On 18 February itself, the news of all what was happening at *Talwar* was known to all the ratings in the Depot but generally the situation was fairly normal. The Commanding Officer, Captain Inigo Jones was on leave and Commander Streatfield was officiating Commanding Officer. At about 0815 hrs, on the morning of 19 February 1946 Captain Inigo Jones when at home was told to assume command of HMIS *Talwar* by FOB. He was aware of the unrest and was mentally prepared when he arrived at the RIN depot. The ratings were shouting slogans. There was mild stone throwing at his arrival by some hot headed sailors. He was talking to his men when a group of ratings from other ships arrived in an agitated mood and wanted the ratings of his establishment to follow them. FOB was informed of the fast changing situation at the Depot. Very soon men from other establishments, shouting slogans, had also started coming to the Depot. The Chief of Staff of FOB instructed the CO to take immediate steps to control entry and exit gates to stop outsiders. At about 1250hrs the naval ensign was hauled down. Slogans were shouted randomly and by evening the Commanding Officer requested FOB for help from the Army and the need for safety of Arms in the armoury.

There were alarming reports of few road side scuffles in and around Fort Barracks. The American flag was removed from the United State Information Service Offices and burnt. A few naval ratings were arrested for acts of hooliganism and placed in naval custody. In the night the ratings from Fort Barrack came to Castle Barracks and wanted these persons to be released. By now all British Officers were advised not to come to Castle Barracks. At 2300 hrs Bombay Area Commander General Beard, Flag Officer Bombay Rear Admiral Rattray and Brigadier Southgate visited Castle Barracks. During the night a broom was hoisted on the Flag Staff mast. The situation had become tense. Past midnight around 150 ratings from HMIS *Hamla*, Landing Craft Establishment at Marve about 20 miles north of Bombay, led by an officer said to be Lieutenant Subhani arrived and forced their entry in the Central Communication Centre located near Castle Barracks. They created a disturbance and also caused some damage to the Centre. FOB was informed and military aid was requested. By 0600 hrs 0n 20 February 1946 a platoon of Maratha Light Infantry was in position. The situation continued to remain tense. No food was prepared in the galley. A lorry full of ratings from *Talwar* drove in. They and their followers in the Depot called all the men to assemble at quarter deck and then informed them about the grievances of the ratings that they had given to the Flag Officer Bombay. In this meeting a president was also elected as a representative of the ratings of Castle Barracks and he went to *Talwar* for better coordination of joint efforts. The situation was now nearly out of control. The staff in the 'Drafting Office' was told to go home. By then two more Maratha platoons had also arrived. The main gate of Castle Barracks was closed. The Army troops had stopped at the gate. They were stoned and all type of objects, like flower pots, iron balls/canon balls were thrown at them by the ratings from the parapets of Castle Barrack. There was repeated demand for removal of Military by the ratings of Castle Barracks. No food was cooked. The ratings wanted to go out for food but were prevented from going out. The situation became so tense that there were moments when these could lead to opening fire on them. Even Khan, President of the striking ratings, who had come to Castle Barracks, could not restrain them to further aggravate it. He fainted while pleading with them.

Action Station - Castle Barracks

On the morning of 20 February the ratings were excited and the normalcy was very fragile. Firstly the ratings in Naval Barracks had asked authorities to give them newspapers. The Newspapers were given but they still were uncertain of coming time. The previous evening they had unloaded some rations given to them but no food was cooked in the galley. Therefore they wanted to go out of barracks for food but the Military Guards did not allow them. Some sailors pleaded with them and showed them their empty stomachs. Having failed, some ratings then broke open the 'Family Canteen' and became unruly, shouting slogans and damaging fittings and fixtures in this area. They were warned by the guards to stop causing damage and behave properly. When the ratings did not stop and continued with hooligan acts, the guards opened fire at them. It was free for all after that. The ratings broke open the ships armoury, armed themselves with rifles and started sniping at the military Guards from elevated parapets of Castle Barracks. They threw anything at the military guards that they could come handy to them. It was said that the ratings threw hand grenades also. By then Brigadier Southgate of Bombay Area had established his Headquarters at Naval Barracks. The situation was now fast turning to a point of no return. The mutineers had also sent a signal to all ships in harbour telling them that if the military guards are not withdrawn they should also open fire.

On 21 February 1946 all civilians working in offices and in the Gun Gate area adjacent to Castle Barracks were told to vacate this area. Gates of Castle Barracks and the area around it was under army control. In the morning the sailors restricted to barracks asked for newspapers. Newspapers were sent to them. Thereafter they wanted to go out for breakfast but were prevented and not allowed to go out. Unruly ratings continued to jostle and insisted on going out. They were warned and when they persisted with their attempts the military guards opened fire on them. The fire was returned by the sailors from the parapets of Castle Barracks. A signal from Castle Barracks was flashed to the ships that they were surrounded by the Military and 20 ratings have died. The situation had now become very grim and the officers on board ships, who were advising restraint to the men on board, were also told to leave the ships. The mutinous ships companies were now manning guns. They had assumed control whilst the naval authority was also acting as per their action plans. It must be said to the credit of the striking ratings that it required the bravest of the brave heart to face the British might in this unequal contest. The ratings were now facing British military might similar to 1857 mutiny against England.

Unrest Spreads

The unrest of naval ratings did not remain confined to barracks and quickly spread to other ships and establishments. The then Flag ship HMIS *Narbada*, the ship of senior-most Naval Officer afloat was also badly affected. Ratings had refused work and the Union Jack was hauled down. Groups of unruly and striking sailors visited other ships, used signals and announced by loud hailers to further widen and spread the unrest to more ships. In these ships the Union Jack and Naval Ensigns were pulled down and the Congress and Muslim League flags were hoisted on the mast heads. By 19 February 1946 the following His Majesty Indian Ships in Bombay were up in arms:-

JUMNA	DHANUSH	MAHRATTA	ASSAM
GONDWANA	BOMBAY	PUNJAB	OUDH
KUMOAN	ORISSA	KARACHI	LAHORE
CUTTAK	NASIK	MADURA	POONA

AMRITSAR and Persian Gun Boats, LAL, NILAH, and HIRA

On 20 February 1946 HMIS *Khyber*, *Patna*, *Agra* and *Kalavati* also joined the mutiny in Bombay. By this time news of naval unrest in Bombay was known in all naval stations. All ships and establishments had raised the banner of revolt except few ships stationed in the Pacific or Trincomellee, (CEYLON, now Sri Lanka) By now, almost all naval ratings had struck work and sympathy strikes were staged at Karachi, Vizagapatnam, Madras, Cochin, Jamnagar and Bahrein. In Jamnagar, sailors went on hunger strike. VALSURA at Jamnagar was late to come to know about strike in Bombay than other naval stations and they were on strike during 25 to 29 February 1946. In Calcutta about 150 ratings went on hunger strike and stopped work. Ominous signs of greater upheaval were looming large and a show down between mutinous ratings and naval administrative authority was imminent. The unrest in sailors in all naval stations was due to their spontaneous reactions to naval administration and the British Naval and Army authorities were busy planning to mercilessly crush it.

In *Talwar*, the naval administration had pre-warning of disaffection of the ratings. Flag Officer Bombay was also aware of the rift and dislike of the ratings for their Commanding Officer, yet he waited till it exploded into open confrontation between them. This situation further aggravated on 16 and 17 February 1946. Thereafter, it was too late to salvage it. By 20 February 1946 the naval ratings had gone on mutiny and this news had spread to all naval stations. At Karachi all under-trainee boys in HMIS *Bahadur*, the Boy's Training Establishment went on hunger strike. Atta used for their meals was found with weevils and unfit for human consumption. The mutiny had now over taken naval service. It, not only was word of mouth or naval channels of communication but the Bombay Press had also played a remarkable role by freely and frankly publishing the news of naval unrest unmindful of protocol of Public Relation Directorate of Defence and at the risk of earning its displeasure.

On 20 February 1946, Castle Barracks had become the nerve centre of anti-naval activities. The sailors from ships in Dock yard and other naval establishments were contacting all places and very often going to *Talwar* for advice from the Central Strike Committee. These sailors were sternly told not to leave Castle Barracks. About 150 sailors were arrested for disobeying this order. The RN Barrack was literally under siege. The news of naval unrest was also beginning to gain the sympathy of the Indian Army and Air Force. Some political parties by now had started openly expressing support to the ratings.

Ships in Bombay harbour - HMIS *Jumna*

Jumna was 4 inch gun sloop and the ratings on board ship were in complete sympathy with the hunger strikers of *Talwar*. On 20 February 1946, they had also gone ashore and taken to the streets along with sailors from other ships/units in Fort Area of Bombay. On 20 February all decks of the ship were decorated with Congress and Muslim League flags. The firing in Naval Barracks was heard. Earlier a signal informing casualties of 20 sailors and the requirement of arms and ammunition had been received on board. This was the moment when all the guns on board were manned by the sailors. The ships have heavy armament on the upper decks but they carry very few small arms on board ship. Due to unavailability of small arms many sailors in other ships had armed themselves with cutlasses from the armoury and even sticks. In these prevailing chaotic circumstances, the dockyard workers also wanted arms and ammunition from ships to be given to them. The armouries were broken open. Sometime later from the back waters, a volley of Oerilikon fire and intermittent firing of small arms was directed towards Naval Barracks by a small Motor Launch to show solidarity with the striking ratings under siege of Army Guards in Castle Barracks. The rattling fire had also enthused ratings on HMIS *Kumoan*, a bigger naval ship. It raised steam and shifted berth to get in position to fire at a RN Ship, HMS *Braganza* also berthed in Bombay harbour.

In this escalating and horrific confrontation between the mutineers and the British forces Flag Officer Bombay Admiral Rattray met Khan, the President of the Central Strike Committee. Khan was going round in the dock area and counselling patience and forbearance among the agitated men in Naval Barracks, on board ships and the Dockyard. It was in this highly surcharged and explosive condition, Flag Officer Bombay met Khan, President of Strike Committee and told him that if the mutiny of the sailors continued the consequences would be very serious and no conditions except unconditional surrender would be considered. It was evident from this oral warning that reconciliatory postures had now given way to open threats. It is understood that during this conversation with FOB Khan had also asked him, "What will happen if the ships fire?" Admiral replied that he would be well prepared to face these consequences and they would be totally obliterated if they persisted to remain defiant. The Flag Officer Bombay was now prepared to face the consequences of failure of his administration. The die was cast and the British Naval authorities appeared in no mood to show any restraint or any more moderation in its pre-planned action, or to seek or initiate any reconciliatory approach, or to find an amicable solution. This was no different to the stance taken earlier by Commander King in HMIS *Talwar* with a view to teach the sailors a lesson. The same policy was to be followed at all naval stations to crush the defiance of ratings at all naval stations.

Action Stations– KARACHI

Shore Establishments - HMIS *Bahadur*

Boys Training Establishment (BTE) in Karachi. After joining naval service, the Boys entry ratings, (under 16 years age), did their basic training in *Bahadur*. It included educational subjects to bring them educationally up to matriculation level. They also did their basic seaman ship training there before joining ships. By now the Boys under trainees were aware of the strike in Bombay. On 20 February 1946 they complained to OOD

(Officer of the Day) that atta was bitter in taste. OOD checked and found weevils in it. Thereafter, all ratings went on hunger strike and they were being kept under watch thereafter.

On 21 February 1946 in the meeting when the Commanding Officer was listening to their grievances some sailors went and lowered the Naval Ensign from the mast. It was torn and they hoisted a 'JAI HIND' flag on the mast in its place. A large group of these Boys first went to other establishments, first to HMIS *Chamak*, a shore establishment, and then to the Himalaya, the Gunnery School at Karachi. They noticed that a 'Bunder' (Naval Ferry) with a large number of sailors from HMIS *Travancore* bound for Keamari was passing by *Bahadur*. It was heading for HMIS *Hindustan*, a 4 inch gun sloop in Karachi harbour. It could be seen from the signal tower of *Bahadur* that 4 inch guns of *Hindustan* were pointing towards BOAC Flying Area and firing at it. Such were these tense and chaotic conditions at Karachi when Flag Officer Commanding Royal Indian Navy (FOCRIN) was addressing the mutineers from All India Radio Bombay and issuing them an ultimatum to unconditionally surrender or perish.

On 22 February the armoury of HMIS *Bahadur* was broken and there were some incidents of small arms firing by the striking sailors. They broke glass panes and damaged few motor vehicles. Next day it was again the same defiance and mutinous conditions that prevailed at these establishments. It was in these conditions that the Naval command was handed over to the Army. It was Lieutenant Colonel Brenson who brought about surrender of these revolting men.

HMIS *Chamak* and HMIS *Himalaya*

Chamak and *Himalaya* were Electrical and Gunnery training establishments. When news of the mutiny broke out the ratings from these two shore establishments joined together with men from Bahadur and wanted to go to HMIS *Hindustan* the ship in harbour with its 4 inch guns at ready. They seized a Landing Craft and were heading towards it when they were intercepted by two Army boats. These boats came along side and after firing a warning shot, opened fire on them. It was a very grim situation indeed.

HMIS *Hindustan*

With the situation quickly slipping out of hand, on 20 February 1946 Naval Headquarters (NHQs) sent a signal and ordered HMIS *Hindustan* and

HMIS *Travancore* to proceed to sea. The news of unrest in Bombay by then was widely known to all men in uniform in all ships and establishments at Karachi. Ships were being prepared for sea when the men on board walked out and these ships could not proceed to sea. These sailors also complained about bad food and collectively voiced their grievance to their commanding officer.

Simultaneously, they also complained about bad behaviour of First Lieutenant a British officer on board *Hindustan*, to the Commanding Officer. It was more like a repeat of the hunger strike incident at HMIS *Talwar*. Their complaint was sent to Captain Cush commanding HMIS *Himalaya* who was the senior most naval officer in Karachi. By the time Captain Cush could initiate any action, he was replaced by Commodore Curtis from Naval Headquarters.

Commodore Curtis was the Senior Administrative Officer (SAO) at Naval Headquarters. He was aware of mass disobedience of sailors fast changing to an open mutiny in the Navy. He was also briefed at GHQ and sent to Karachi as Naval Officer-In-Charge Karachi (NOIC). By then complaints of food and bad behaviour of British naval officers were still remaining unattended. On 21 February, only 3 sailors were permitted to meet the new NOIC Karachi but he could not be contacted and the meeting of the sailors with him did not take place. Two landing crafts packed with ratings coming to HMIS *Hindustan* from other naval establishments were fired upon by two military boats. These boats were first seemed to escort them but later fired at them. This unprovoked incident of firing appeared to have led to 4 inch gun firing by HMIS *Hindustan* in retaliation. Oerlikons guns on board were also fired. It was an armed mutiny by the ratings in Karachi.

Commodore Curtis came on board HMIS *Hindustan*. There was complete confusion on the ship. He addressed the men and told them to surrender unconditionally. He then gave ultimatum to the ratings that if they don't accept surrender to naval authority then the Military would be called to force them to surrender. The time limit of this ultimatum given to the ratings had expired but the ratings on board HMIS *Hindustan* did not obey this order. During this ongoing tussle, the Army had brought and positioned field guns at vantage locations, the non firing areas of naval guns. The guns on *Hindustan* could not fire at them. From the quay side an Army Officer made the announcement that only five minutes would be given to them to decide. They were also told to immediately surrender unconditionally and leave their arms on board. This warning also cautioned them that in case anyone was seen on the upper deck he would be fired upon with small arm. It was such a belligerent face of British administration that provoked and intimidated those ratings who complained of food or bad behaviour of the First Lieutenant, a Royal Naval Officer. The conciliatory approach, like in Bombay, had been abandoned. The challenge to the ratings was humiliating and caused greater anger and hate for naval authorities. Under this feeling of desolation, they retaliated and opened fire with 4 inch guns and other weapons on board HMIS *Hindustan*. The Army returned fire with 75 mm Howitzers and mortars. Technically the ratings could have matched the fire power of the Army but guns on ship could not be depressed enough to aim at them. The ratings were indeed technically not competent and this shortcoming was fully exploited to the hilt by the clever naval administration. In this one sided match of gun fire between expert army gunners and novice junior ratings on board ship, the conclusion was foregone. After getting repeated hits the firing by the guns of HMIS *Hindustan* ceased and the ship surrendered. This gun battle went on for 20 minutes. HMIS *Hindustan* was badly damaged and suffered many causalities. The damage to the ship was beyond economical repairs and it did not re-join naval service thereafter.

CIVIL UNREST

At Bombay

The report of the hunger strike by the sailors at HMIS *Talwar* on 18 February went around the city of Bombay like wild fire. It evoked considerable sympathy spontaneously from the civilian port and dock workers and they demanded justice for these ratings. On 19 February more than 2000 ratings had marched in procession in the streets of Bombay and held a meeting at Azad Maidan. The Civilian Port and Dock workers unions also staged a strike and came on the streets taking out processions and shouting slogans. Late on the night of 20-21 February 1946 and on 21 February there were wide-spread disturbances and disorder in the city of Bombay. All mill hands, railway workers and all odd and sundry workers in port area struck work. They took out procession through the streets of Bombay shouting slogans. Complete unrest prevailed in entire Fort area. Banks were attacked and there were many cases of looting in the Fort area. By the night of 22 February the civil unrest in Bombay had gained momentum and the situation further deteriorated in Mill Areas. Curfew was imposed in Bombay. Many shops were looted or burnt. The impact of mass unrest in Bombay could be seen from the fact that of 75 mills in the area 71 were on strike. Many streets were barricaded and railway lines were also reported to have been tampered with. The police, assisted by military armoured cars, fired on unruly mobs on numerous occasions and considerable blood spilled on to the streets of Bombay. Curfew Order was proclaimed as the whole city of Bombay was in a state of turmoil.

At Karachi

There was unrest in Karachi town and it further deteriorated to such an extent that at many times the police had to resort to the use of tear gas shells to disperse the crowds. Army troops were also called out and they were standing by with the police to keep the situation under control. In these conditions a unit of Royal Indian Air Force (RIAF) at Drigh Road refused duty and all Airmen were placed under close arrest.

At Calcutta

More than 400 naval ratings in Calcutta refused to work. They went on strike to sympathize with the ratings that had resorted to mutiny and were continuing to defy naval authorities along with others supportive civilian personnel who were still actively continuing the strike in Bombay and Karachi. With a view to contain building up of the unruly and disruptive situation in Calcutta and its suburbs the assembly of men in public meetings was prohibited. These prohibitory orders were however withdrawn for the public meeting that was being held in an open 'maidan' by supporters of the Muslim League. This favourable change in policy by the State Government was stated to be so decided because it was the view of these authorities that large crowds of people would attend this meeting and would not take to the streets to support the mutiny by naval ratings in Calcutta. This meeting was being addressed by Mr. MA Jinnah President of the Muslim League. There was no wide spread rioting but trams and bus services were stopped. At Howrah and Sealdah railway stations trains were also prevented to move by left wing elements. The main political parties appeared to avoid taking part in these disturbances but large groups of students were noticed being instigated by Communists party workers.

Counter Action

During the war, the complaints of food and other service matters were faced by the naval administration but after the war these had snowballed into open mutiny in the Navy. There were a number of cases of hunger strikes in many naval units but the concerned commanding officers chose to summarily punish the strikers rather than investigate, correct the malady and do justice to their complainants. Such cases of injustice to men and short comings in administration in the service were known to higher naval administration but instead of remedying the cause of their complaints the senior naval command chose to ignore these for reasons best known to them. But this indifferent practice encouraged them to sweep these types of complaints of ratings under the carpet and sternly control them by application of naval discipline. Commander King also adopted the same technique in HMIS *Talwar* after the war. In short "Might was Right" was the rule practiced in the navy. This maxim perhaps was tolerated by those ratings during war time under stress of war time contingencies. But in the post war atmosphere, the ratings were in no mood to accept and bear with this injustice. Further, the anticipation of freedom was evident in India and ongoing trials of INA personnel gave new meaning to the naval ratings and their aspirations.

It is a common saying that tyrannical and dictatorial practices die hard and the naval authorities, in an authoritarian manner, chose to follow the good old war time practice and did its best to crush the threatening mutiny of naval ratings by browbeating them with the naval discipline act against those who led them to a mutiny. Their wide displacements kept Indian armed forces far apart from each other during war but now a sympathy wave for their comrade in arms, the striking naval ratings, infused spirit de corps in some army units and a unit in the RIAF and they also went on a sympathy strike. A quick crushing and punitive military action became imminent to control this rapidly growing wild fire of mutiny of naval ratings and it now was deployment of the Army to quell this mutiny in naval ranks. The ratings were no match to this unequal contest.

Change of Command

In Great Britain Royal Navy had been always regarded as the senior service. In keeping with this tradition the Royal Indian Navy was ceremoniously the senior service in India as well, but placed under His Excellency, General Auchinleck, Commander-in-Chief in India, General Headquarters (GHQ) at Delhi. After consultations at GHQs, Flag Officer Commanding (FOC RIN), Admiral (Retd) JH Godfrey had requested Commander-in-Chief East Indies for help. Heavy cruiser HMS *Glasgow* along with all possible available help was urgently requested to be sent to Bombay as the sailor's mutiny was becoming very menacing. The command of the Navy in all naval stations was then transferred to the Army. On 20 February 1946, General Lockhart commanding southern command and General O' Conner GOC-in-C, Southern Command took over command of all naval stations in Bombay. They held detailed discussions with local naval authorities in their respective Area HQs and the military action became imminent.

Broadcast by FOCRIN

On 20 February 1946 a large number of ratings in naval uniforms but with no caps had paraded in the streets and on the roads of Bombay. Flag Officer Bombay issued an order asking all ratings to return to their ships/ establishments by 1530hrs failing which they would be arrested. At 1430hrs military pickets were in position and troops posted outside HMIS *Talwar* and Castle Barracks. About 150 ratings who did not go to their ships were arrested after 1530hrs. There was an exchange of fire between mutineers and army units in Castle Barracks during the day. Tense and under siege, the ratings spent a night of uncertainty with military guards stationed outside their establishments. On 21 February Flag Officer Bombay, with the concurrence of FOCRIN, issued instructions to all naval officers to leave their ships. Naval officers had left, the civilian staff was already withdrawn and now the sailors were stranded in their establishments. The show of force would help demoralize the isolated ratings. When these instructions were being issued at 1300hrs a formation of 20 Royal Air Force (RAF) air craft flew over Bombay harbour. The war time conditions prevailed and in this intimidating and threatening backdrop, FOCRIN was recording his address on AIR to sternly warn the ratings. This address was an ultimatum to them and they were being told to either unconditionally surrender or perish. His broadcast was relayed from All India Radio Station Bombay at 1745hrs. The text of his address reads,

> *"In the present regrettable state of indiscipline in the service, I have adopted this means of addressing RIN as being the way in which I can speak to the greatest number of you at one time.*

To start with, everyone of you must realize that the Government of India has no intention of allowing indiscipline to continue or its actions to be influenced by indiscipline. It will take the most stringent measures to restore discipline using the vast forces at its disposal if necessary. I ask you to bear in mind in considering the other things which I have to say to you now.

As regards the requests made by those of you who waited on Flag Officer Bombay on Tuesday, 10 February you may be assured that all reasonable complaints, grievances, if any, will be fully investigated. Demobilization will proceed strictly in accordance with service groups, though you must realize that this will mean that the Service will lose the trained nucleus of experienced ratings, especially in the Communication Branch.

The whole question of pay, travelling allowances, family allowances, is now being examined by an Inter Service Committee. This Committee has just been afloat in one of HMI ships and visited establishments in Karachi, Jamnagar and Bombay. The situation in Bombay this moring both ashore and afloat is deplorable. A state of open mutiny prevails in which ratings appear to have completely lost control of their senses.

In order to ensure that the ratings confined to barracks did actually stay there and to avoid recurrence of the unfortunate incidents of the day before, it was necessary to place small guards of soldiers at gates of Talwar and Castle Barracks last night.

This morning the ratings from Castle Barracks burst through the guards which were forced to open fire. This fire was replied to by the ratings inside the Barracks. The only reason for firing in the first place was to contain the ratings within the Barracks and not to coerce or intimidate them.

I want again to make it plain that the Government of India will never give in to violence. To continue the struggle is the height of folly when you take into account the overwhelming forces at the disposal of the Government at this time, and will be used to their utmost even if it means the destruction of the Navy of which you have been so proud."

On 20 February when firing was resorted to by the Army troops in Castle Barracks some naval ratings had approached Sardar Patel, member of the Congress Working Committee for help but he declined to interfere. There were wide spread disturbances in the city and on 22 Feb, he sent the following message to the naval mutineers.

"The strikers should lay down all arms and should go through the formality of surrender and the Congress would do its level best to see that there is no victimization and the legitimate demands of naval ratings are met as soon as possible."

This advice was eventually accepted.

The reinforcements to supplement military forces had arrived in Bombay and assistance was also being provided to the civil power to bring normalcy in city. In spite of proclamation of the curfew in the area some cases of civil disturbance did take place. The office of the Communist Party published their manifesto thanking the public for their support whilst alleging atrocities by military personnel when dealing with the striking workers. The naval strike committee of the ratings had met Sardar Patel who was in favour of discontinuing the defiance of naval authority and advised them to surrender. In Bombay this advice was eventually accepted by the sailors. The ships in Bombay harbour hoisted white flags. Following this on the morning of Saturday, 23 February 1946 the ratings in nearly all other naval stations, Karachi, Madras, Vizagapatnam, and Calcutta also surrendered unconditionally. (See Annexure II)

The mutiny had thus ended after having run a course of six days but the smoke of the mutiny kept on smouldering in many units till it was put out with disciplinary actions against agitating personnel. Such was the impact and consequences of the naval mutiny of sailors that also led to civil disturbances in many places intensifying the urge for independence and helped in the early departure of British rulers from India. Following incidents during and following naval mutiny had also unnerved British administration in India.

a) In Gujrat-Kathiawar the train services remained disrupted.

b) Over 1500 British Other Ranks (BOR) of Royal Electrial and Mechanical Engineering (REME) service, were awaiting embarkation to England for a long period. They were angry and gave strike notice to their Station Commander alleging disparity with airmen of the Royal Air Force who had secured early repatriation by unjustified means.

c) The men of the Royal Indian Air Force at Allahabad, Poona, Jodhpur and Madras refused to work.

d) One group of Army personnel belonging to Indian Pioneer Corps refused work and demanded more pay, better food, early release and good civil employment.

e) Indian Other Ranks and many temporarily employed civilians working in military workshops at Secundrabad stopped work

f) Some men of the Maratha Battalion at Kamptee voiced their grievances but there was no connection with demands of the sailors in Bombay

g) Men at the Signal Training Centre at Jabbulpore broke out and paraded in the city.

h) Many men of the Signal Corps at Allahabad also refused duty.

11

Mutiny, a Serious Question

Mutiny is a highly serious battle and a very risky affair, both for the mutineers who stage it and the authority that faces it. During the war, there was no armed confrontation between the sailors and the naval officers although the British naval officers faced many minor mutinies on board some ships and establishments. The 1946 naval mutiny had no new unforeseen elements that the naval administration was not familiar with. The discontent among the sailors for bad service conditions, rotten victuals and consequential hunger strikes as well as the arrogant behaviour of officers were well-known to the naval authorities. Many Commanding Officers had faced these situations during the war and such incidents were always summarily dealt with by the administrative authorities. The eruption of trouble in HMIS *Talwar* also followed the same pattern but now the sailors were also additionally facing an uncertain and bleak future after leaving naval service. The sailors, once submissive, had strengthened themselves to face new challenges in the civil life after the release from the service. This bit of extra zeal and spirit encouraged them to no longer compromise with the inadequacies in the naval service. Though many Commanding Officers, on numerous occasions during the war might have faced similar situations and summarily dealt with the discontented men under them, the men now were more resolute. The old autocratic and oppressive practices were no longer fearsome factors but the heady naval administration still believed so and did not hesitate to further tighten the screw on the undisciplined ratings through their much prejudiced and intolerant new Commanding Officer. The sailors were now more actively and resolutely representing their grievances. Some ratings had written subversive slogans on the eve of the Navy Day to voice their discontentment. The new Commanding Officer, Commander King had successfully caught the alleged ring leader L Tel BC Dutt and was arrogantly pompous about the momentary calm after his arrest. His success was like a flash in the pan because some more incidents took place later and he failed to gauge the intensity of the discontentment that was fast turning into a bigger defiance and an ultimate mutiny in the navy. Like the proverbial Nero who was fiddling while Rome was burning, all this was occurring in HMIS *Talwar* when the new Commanding Officer and the Flag Officer Bombay were fully seized with the problems of the sailors in this establishment.

Commander King had a remarkable success in catching the ring leader soon after his appointment and it must have helped him gain the confidence of the Flag Officer Bombay and his staff officers. This singular success vouched for his administrative ability as compared to the previous command by Lieutenant Commander Coles and his team of officers. After winning the confidence of the naval command, it was now his task to tone up the administration in *Talwar* and to deal with the unruly personnel. Unfortunately, it was his grandiose and ostentatiously overbearing attitude that would have also made the officers and the senior sailors to stay clear. As a result, the staff under him was not pulling together as one unit. His overrated confidence and the methods of administration conveyed the message, 'Boss is always right.' There was no cohesion and the administration was isolated. The whispering and the muted discussions among the men were critical of the bullying and foul mouthing by Commander King towards the ratings and evoked sympathy for the cause of the striking sailors. In no case should have the Commanding Officer been bullying and foul mouthing the off duty watch sailors in the barracks. All felt deeply hurt and were sympathetic to the cause of the agitating ratings. Even the senior sailors were of the view that the foul language used by the Commanding Officer was deeply hurting. It was fairly likely that had the abusive language not been used towards sailors then perhaps these ratings could have been pacified and might not have resorted to mutiny against the naval authorities.

Commanding Officer is regarded as a father figure in any unit. The arrogant and indifferent attitude of the new Commanding Officer not only lowered the stature of his appointment but also added insult to the rank and file of the communication branch. It has always been a well-accepted and standard practice in the navy to appoint professionally qualified officers as Commanding Officers of their Professional Training Establishments. It helped to greatly enhance professional efficiency, instilled *'Esprit de corps'* and forged great affinity amongst men of the same profession in the naval service. Primarily, it was this *Esprit de corps* which united all agitating personnel in the communication branch and also attracted the junior sailors from all departments in all the ships and naval establishments to chart the course of the 1946 mutiny of the sailors in the navy.

Almost everyone in India firmly believed that Indian independence was achieved by popular mass 'Satyagraha' movements led by Mahatma Gandhi. These movements against the British were made possible by the non-violent defiance of British rule in India. *'Satyagraha and Ahimsa'* were morally very strong and superior means of collective protests and defiance against the British authority. There was another section of the Indian leadership that believed that a well-planned and organized armed struggle could hasten the departure of the British from India. Britain had faced both. Firstly, it was the non-violent civil disobedience by the main political parties and then the organized armed struggle by the Indian National Army (INA) soldiers, who had fought the Second World War in the battlefields of Burma for the British Crown. During the war itself, these Indian soldiers in the Japanese Prisoner of War camps had discarded and severed all connections with the Indian Army and under the charismatic leadership of Netaji Subash Chandra Bose formed into fighting units of the INA and fought against the British forces for the liberation of India. After the defeat of Japan, they were taken as British Prisoners of War and awaiting their trials in India. Their heroic spirit of Indian Nationalism and the gallant armed struggle for freedom of India is highly acknowledged and admired by every Indian. Their fight for the liberation of their motherland was the most inspiring. It was in the shadow of these prevailing conditions in India that the unrest in the navy was fast turning into an open revolt against the British naval authority.

Sailors Mutiny – A Historical Event

The Royal Indian Navy was a small fighting force and mostly stationed at two major Indian ports, Bombay and Karachi. Like the vicious British trained INA soldiers, the revolt by the Indian sailors posed no such threat but it held a strong political potential. British statesmanship is par excellence. When the INA was at the gates of India, it was understood that some political understanding emerged between the Indian polity and the leadership of the British Labour Party. The British were ready to grant concessions if the Indian leadership put its weight behind the British war effort. In such political complexities, the decisive moment that sealed the fate of British colonial rule in India and transformed the Indian freedom struggles, was the Mutiny by the Royal Indian Navy in February 1946. Nothing much has been written about this but the understanding of getting concessions, albeit Indian independence was understood to be mooted during the INA uprising also. The naval mutiny was the ultimate bargaining settlement for Indian freedom. It is a forgotten chapter in the Indian history for neither the British nor Indian nationalist historians had written much about it. The fact remains that the 1946 mutiny was a crucial turning point in the Indian history.

On 26 February 1946 Mr. Attlee, the then British Prime Minister, made a statement in the House of Commons regarding the Indian Naval Mutiny, lending his support and justifying the actions of General Claude Auchinleck, Commander-in-Chief in India and a stern warning of attack by land, sea and air forces issued on All India Radio by FOCRIN. He also mentioned about the civil disturbances in India. Mr Attlee declared in the house that both the Congress and Muslim League leaders cooperated in condemning the mutiny and made efforts to stop the disturbances. However, the Communist Party have issued a manifesto thanking the public for its support to the mutinous ratings.

Great Show of Force

During the war, Indian naval ships were deployed for harbour defence duties. Its oceangoing sloops, fitted with twin four inch guns on hand operated gun mountings were also performing escort duties. The fighting efficiency of a ship is a team work of the specialized and trained personnel from many departments. No single department can sail and wage a sea battle. The junior naval ratings who had gone on mutiny were neither capable of sailing a ship nor engaging in a sea battle. At the most, they wielded the threat of firing a gun salvo or two, aimlessly beyond the safety firing arcs of the guns on the ships in harbour and their guns were unable to fire at close range land targets. The two ships, HMIS *Hindustan* and HMIS *Jamuna*, fitted with four inch guns were the main fire power of the mutinous sailors but both were also landlocked and easy targets for close range army artillery. HMIS *Jamuna* had fired aimlessly and HMIS *Hindustan* was disabled by the shore based army mortar fire. No outside assistance was essentially required to neutralize the armed naval threat from the sailors. But the Flag Officer Commanding RIN (FOCRIN) requested Commander-in-Chief (C-in-C), East Indies to send help hastily in concurrence with the Commander-in-Chief of India. Consequently, heavy cruiser HMS *Glasgow* and seven other fleet ships, Carron, Ness, Halladale, Loch quoich, Cavalier, Petard and Loch more, an invincible naval task force, was heading to Bombay to fight the ill-armed and ill- trained junior sailors incapable of waging a sea battle. With India knocking at the doors of independence, the great sea force might have been assembled not merely to tame rebellious junior sailors but also to overawe simmering political disdain and superiority.

Naval personnel are not required to engage in hand combat, therefore, ships do not carry a sizeable number of small arms on board. With the available small arms on board, armed sailors could hold Commanding Officers and other officers as hostage, but during the mutiny no such case was reported. Simple minded sailors were not wily or scheming tacticians. They were collectively agitating for the rightful dues before their release. The release from the service is a period in the life of every service man when he feels unshackled from the service discipline. In such circumstances, few may have strayed and been affected by the political fervour prevailing then in the country. L Tel BC Dutt who was a bit politically active was the spring board of this struggle in HMIS *Talwar* and also author of a book on this subject which he very appropriately titled 'Mutiny of the Innocents.'

Leaderless but now not so innocent sailors who broke the Naval Discipline Act faced an entire war machine of the British War Office in India. The Royal Indian Naval authorities had proved to be ineffective to control their men and thus handed over the command of the navy to General Claude Auchinleck, Commander-in-Chief of India. Before this, on 18 February 1946, the Flag Officer Bombay held a meeting with the sailors, and assured them that their grievances would be looked into and asked them to select their committee and elect their leader. Their service grievances could have been addressed whilst personnel demanding issues of political nature could perhaps have been segregated. Management of men was not a naval forte and the morale and security of the naval personnel became the responsibility of army officers. On 19 February 1946, Commander King was removed and Captain Inigo Jones was appointed the Commanding Officer. It was thus substantiated that not only had Commander King failed but he helped aggravate discontentment in the men under him. It was a failure of command before the sailors took to the streets. The sailors were no match against a war tested British military machine. First, they were isolated in their barracks in all the naval stations and then forced to surrender unconditionally.

All preparations had been made by the authorities. It was time to execute the plan and overwhelm the mutineers. The ultimatum given to the ratings in all the naval stations to unconditionally surrender was the first step to dishearten and demoralize them. During the period between 18 - 21 February 1946, senior naval officers, Rear Admiral Rattray in Bombay and Commander Gush in Karachi, were trying to placate the sailors in their respective stations and verbally assuring them that their grievances would be suitably redressed. To pacify the ruffled feelings of the sailors in HMIS *Talwar*, their deviant commanding officer, Commander King was replaced by a very senior naval officer, Captain Inigo Jones. The Flag Officer Bombay also visited the ships in the Bombay harbour with L Sig Khan, president of the Strike Committee assuring the agitated sailors but simultaneously deployed the army personnel in all the disturbed areas. While the sailors were being persuaded in this manner, the radio conversations between the defiant ships and the other units were being continuously monitored to compel them to an unconditional surrender.

Very soon, the naval authorities knew that the ships were experiencing an acute shortage of food and water. Many ships in Bombay did not have ammunition on board for its main armament as ships normally 'de ammunition' before berthing in the harbour. By 21 February 1946, from the intercepted communication between the ships, the naval authorities knew that sailors on ships cannot open fire with the main armament on these ships. The guns on ships might have given raw courage to the sailors but the guns on ships were literally ineffective in the real battle. These ships were thus sitting ducks and easy targets. It was from this strategically well-placed position that FOCRIN, Admiral Godfrey gave an ultimatum of unconditional surrender to the sailors by broadcasting on the All India Radio on the evening of 20 February 1946 as the army units moved to their designated positions.

The action plan was unfolding and from Delhi Commodore, Curtis, who had arrived in Karachi just before the radio broadcast, had been fully briefed accordingly. He replaced Commander Gush, a senior Naval Officer in Charge, Karachi who was scheduled to listen to the grievances of the ratings and address them. Commodore Curtis neither addressed the sailors nor listened to their grievances. Such was the contempt for the sailors and their demands. HMIS *Hindustan* became the main centre of naval resistance in Karachi. Commodore Curtis went on board HMIS *Hindustan* and told the striking ship' company and its ratings who assembled on board from other establishments to surrender unconditionally. While he was addressing them, a British army unit already took up position in the harbour to engage and overpower HMIS *Hindustan* if it refused to comply.

British Army authorities were all set to ruthlessly crush the mutiny of the junior ratings of the Royal Indian Navy. The ultimatum to unconditionally surrender had already been aired on All India Radio Bombay. Bravado of the ratings turned into extreme anxiety. The deadline set for surrender had expired and soon firing had commenced. HMIS *Jamuna* in Bombay fired 4 inch gun salvo aimlessly and ratings on board *Hindustan* in Karachi fired from their 4 inch guns to put up brave fight against the well positioned British armoured units sent to subdue it. The firing lasted for just over 20 minutes. The ship was totally crippled and the sailors accepted to surrender unconditionally. That was the end of the sailor's mutiny in Karachi.

After the address of FOCRIN on 21 February 1946 in Bombay, there were hectic consultations between the men on board ships and the sailors ashore in the evening. The President of the Strike Committee, MS Khan was shore based and the sailors on board ships feeling utterly defenceless were highly nervous. They decided to accept unconditional surrender but some ratings in the Castle Barracks had earlier acquired small arms from armouries and resisted for a short period. Finding themselves pitted against a vastly superior force, they finally agreed to surrender their weapons. All the ships hoisted white flags. On 23 February 1946 at 0600 hrs, mutiny of sailors ended in unconditional surrender. A short and crisp, immediate RIN General message **IG 479** addressed to the First Sea Lord and the other British authorities at London that read **"RIN mutiny at Bombay has ended"** was flashed by the Flag Officer commanding the Royal Indian Navy. Mop up operations followed in Bombay but in some other naval stations in India, defiance continued a little longer.

Smouldering Discontent

Bombay

Following the surrender, all the ships in the harbour and main establishments in Bombay area were put under the military guard. Soon after the surrender, the process of collection of arms, ammunition and immobilization of ships began by 24 February 1946. A few stray incidents of disobedience continued to be reported from some outlying units. 200

ratings of HMIS *Hamla*, a shore establishment in Bombay, refused to surrender. They were segregated and placed under the military custody.

Hunger strike was also reported from a detention camp of sailors at Mulund in Bombay. This hunger strike continued till 14 March 1946 and finally the last sign of revolt by the naval ratings against the injustice of British naval administration had ended.

Karachi

After the surrender at Bombay, the situation in Karachi further deteriorated and spread to the Royal Indian Air Force (RIAF). Mortar firing by an army shore battery completely damaged HMIS *Hindustan* beyond repair. All the sailors on board the ship were taken into close custody.

Andaman

HMIS *Kistna* based in the far off isle of Andaman reported a strike on board and 'no cooperation' by the men in manning the ship.

Bahrain

Men at the Naval Signal Station Bahrain defied the orders and refused to carry out their duties.

Jubbulpore and Allahabad

Most army personnel from the Army Signal Centre at Jubbulpore and Signal Corps at Allahabad took out processions and refused to perform duties.

Governor's Reports

Politically, India was highly surcharged but no Indian political party openly supported the cause of the 1946 sailors' mutiny. However, it was largely expected that some political elements might have contacted the disgruntled sailors. Few of these sailors might have gone around and associated with certain sections of the political activists. Not only the British military authority but also the civil administration in all the affected naval stations constantly monitored the civil disturbances that erupted in sympathy and support of the sailor's unrest in Bombay. Though the mutiny of the sailors was purely a defence service matter, it had political repercussions also.

The Indian population awakened and the leadership of all the Indian political parties had formulated its own political path for the independence of India from the British Crown. The goal was the same but the philosophies behind their political movements were different. Each party had nurtured its own area of influence and mass appeal. It was most likely that a few naval sailors were swayed away by outside political elements and looked for help to their cause. Likewise, some of these political elements would have found in the agitation of the naval sailors an opportunity to gain politically. Few sailors were swayed away by such political connivance and formed a closely knit group. Their subversive activities in the naval units mocked at the naval authorities and helped create further disaffection in naval personnel. A combined civilian political struggle along with the mutinous naval personnel in many naval stations would have posed a formidable challenge to the British Government.

According to rules of the defence service, armed forces personnel are not permitted to associate or take part in any shade or type of political activity. It is a common and a uniform policy in all armed forces. The defaulters were given severe punishments. It was the tallest Indian political leader, Shri Subash Chandra Bose who decimated this well ingrained strict discipline in the Indian armed forces and re-inculcated the spirit of Indian freedom in the Indian soldiers taken as Prisoner of War by Japan during World War II. After their defeat, these INA soldiers, now prisoners of war in the British Barracks in Red Fort were awaiting trial in Delhi when the mutiny of the sailors erupted in Bombay.

The British Government was also fully alive to these developments taking place in the country. The provincial Governors were alive to this threat and took suitable remedial measures to prevent the naval mutiny from turning into an all India agitation. They were fully alive to the significant political pressures and constraints on account of the naval unrest and weathered prevailing political contingencies and expediencies, in their respective provinces. The Governor's report generally pertained to the incidents of law and order situations indicative of any overtone of sympathy with the mutiny of sailors in the navy. Their reports also included observations from the political angle and attitude of the Indian political parties. Their reports clearly indicated propensity and tendencies of various political parties towards the on-going mutiny of the sailors. A gist of their reports clearly reflected the political disposition in the country.

(a) **BOMBAY** – HMIS *Talwar* in Bombay was the epicentre of the naval mutiny. Whilst General Officer Commanding (GOC) of the Army's Southern Command sent military situation reports to the Commander-in-Chief at Delhi, the Governor of Bombay addressed his reports to the Secretary of State and the Viceroy of India. These reports mentioned that the situation appeared to be well in hand. Mutineers were restricted and mainly confined to the barracks but the striking sailors on board some small ships were well covered by fortress guns. These reports also indicated that:-

(i) Congress officially disowned any participation in the mutiny of the sailors but many left wing elements and communist organizations were trying to work up sympathy and there was sizeable trouble due to the mill hands and transport workers.

(ii) Communists and the student wing of the Congress had staged demonstrations in the city.

(iii) A few Congress and Muslim League leaders were interviewed. They deplored the disturbances and disowned responsibility. They said that they did their best to restore normalcy.

(b) **BENGAL** – Around 400 sailors in sympathy with the incidents in Bombay and Karachi had refused work. Traders were agitated and went on strike against the sales tax. Trams were not running partly due to internal troubles within the operating company and this situation aggravated due to the Communist propaganda. Suitable prohibitory orders under the Police Act were promulgated.

An election meeting to be addressed by Mohammad Ali Jinnah, the President of the Muslim League was scheduled to be held on Sunday, 24 February 1946. This meeting was attended by a large number of Muslims and this passed off peacefully. It gave a clear impression that leaders of the main Indian political parties were anxious to avoid disturbances. They however had their own difficulties in restraining students who were being incited by the Communist workers.

(c) **SIND** - At Karachi, both the Congress and the Communist parties held meetings showing sympathy towards the naval sailors on strike. The Communists made inciting speeches but the Congress observed restraint. All the public meetings were prohibited but both the parties did not obey these orders.

(d) **MADRAS** –

   (i) There were strikes and a number of incidents of disturbances in the city to show sympathy with the naval sailors on mutiny.

   (ii) The workers strike had spread to the Buckingham Carnatic Mills. Strikers were inspired by the Communists taking to the streets in sympathy with the RIN ratings. Local Congress leaders also went on strike but appealed for non-violence.

(e) **CENTRAL PROVINCE** -- There were incidents of disturbances and strikes at two stations in the province.

At Jubbulpore, the Army Signal Training School was apparently affected due to the strike by the communication centres, civilian riots in Bombay and trail of INA personnel at Delhi. The army personnel came out of their barracks and took out processions carrying the flags of the Congress, the Muslim League and the Communist parties. They also held public meetings.

Echo of Naval Mutiny in Central Assembly

The news of the sailor mutiny featured regularly in the press. The nation was shocked but the mutiny was a defining moment in the Indian history. After the INA, the junior sailors of the navy had now openly defied the British Crown. It was an indication enough that Britain could no longer hold India in slavery with the Indian forces like it did in the past. The English and the Vernacular Press regularly covered and reported the events of the naval mutiny. The Public Relations Directorate of the General Headquarters of India issued regular press communiqués. Indian national leadership was also seized and keenly concerned with the consequences of the mutiny of sailors in Bombay and the other naval stations. They tabled many questions in the Indian Assembly and wanted these to be answered by the Government. On 22 February 1946, when the mutiny was raging and the action plan to snuff it out swiftly and ruthlessly was approved and initiated, Mr. Mason, Joint Secretary, War Department made the following statement in the Assembly in replying to the short notice questions on the strikes at Bombay and Karachi:

Sir, I have three questions on this subject and two of them are of the same length. If you give me permission, Sir, I propose to reply by lengthy statements in which I will state the information that we have up to date on the whole subject.

*On Monday the 18 February at 1200 hrs, that is mid-day, serious trouble broke out in HMIS Talwar, the RIN Signal School in Bombay. All ratings, except Chief Petty officers and Petty officers, refused duty and refused to listen to their officers. The Establishment includes about 1100 ratings. The Flag Officer Bombay at once took over the charge of this Establishment himself and visited it but he was unable to find out what the men's grievances were. FOB came to the conclusion, however, that the Commanding Officer of HMIS Talwar should be replaced and he was replaced by a senior and experienced officer. On Tuesday 19 Feb, the trouble spread to RIN Depot and Castle Barracks Bombay, and the ships in Bombay Harbour. There was considerable rowdyism in the streets and civil police made arrests of some ratings involved in acts of violence. During the course of this day, FOB visited Talwar and met 14 ratings who came forward as leaders or spokesmen, and then for the **first time** he found out what the demands of the men were. They were,*

1.   *No victimisation of the so called strikers.*

2.   *Release of RK Singh TEL from Arthur Road Prison immediately. (RK Singh was due to be released but instead he requested Commander King, the Commanding Officer to accept his resignation from the Service and was punished with imprisonment).*

3.   *Speedy mobilization according to age and service group with reasonable peace time employment.*

4.   *Immediate disciplinary action against Commander King for his behaviour and insulting language used by him to the personnel of HMIS Talwar.*

5.   *The best class of Indian food.*

6.   *Royal Navy scale of pay, family allowance and travelling facilities and use of NAAFI stores.*

7.   *No kit to be taken from Indian Navy personnel at the time of release.*

8. *Immediate grant of war gratuity and treasury pay on release.*

9. *Good behaviour of officers towards lower deck men.*

10. *Quicker promotions of lower deck men to officers and all new officers coming from abroad are to be stopped.*

11. *New Commanding Officer for HMIS Talwar. Commander Cole previous Commanding Officer is reappointed.*

12. *All demands to be decided by authorities through a national leader whose name will be given.*

The Committee of ratings also wished to make protest to GOI regarding (a) INA policy, (b) Firing on the public in various places and the use of Indian troops in the Middle East and Near East.

On the 19 February some 120 ratings in Calcutta staged, what was described, as a sit-down mutiny with some what similar demands. During the night 150 ratings led by an officer proceeded from Marve to Bombay and tried to break into the Central Communication Office. They were not successful and were locked up on their return to Marve. On Wednesday, the 20 February there were no serious rioting during the morning although the streets were crowded with ratings who refused to do their duty or obey orders. The Flag Officer Bombay, who issued a message in the afternoon, which was read verbally, to all establishments and ships companies by their Commanding Officers and announced in the harbour by loud hailers . This ordered all ratings to be in their ship or establishment by 1530hrs after which anyone found outside would be liable to be arrested.

By this time the mutiny had spread to other establishments in the neighborhood of Bombay but in these establishments the ratings were not and were still not using violence. It is notable also that the dockyard workmen had refused to join the trouble.

On the 21 February at 2140 hrs the ratings who in accordance with arrangements of 20 February were confined to barracks, began to try to break out of their barracks and guards from Maratha Light Infantry who were posted at the barracks were compelled to open fire which they did with a single shot. The guard was stoned by the ratings who had obtained rifles and ammunition and returned their fire. Shortly afterwards a report was received that ships in harbour were raising steam in order to hoist ammunition for 4 inch guns. Rifle fire from ships to shore continued during the morning and few rounds of light shell fire, I think, from two small guns which fire small shells were fired towards the town. One shell caused injuries to several civilians.

At 1430hrs the Flag Officer Bombay proceeded to the dockyard and met the leaders of the mutineers to whom he gave a very serious warning telling them that no conditions other than unconditional surrender would be accepted, that the troops in no circumstances would be withdrawn and overwhelming force would be brought to bear if the mutineers proceeded in their present attitude. The Flag Officer Commanding broadcast the message about the same time a message, which probably all members have seen in the newspapers this morning.

Sri M Annathasayanam Ayyangar:- A threat.

Mr M R Masani :- Disgraceful.

Diwan Chaman Lal :- Offering to blow up the Navy

Mr P Mason: *After that the cease fire order was hoisted and there was no more firing from the ships during the afternoon but later in the afternoon there was sporadic outburst of firing in the Castle Barrack area. There are, however, indications that the situation is still very serious. An outbreak of indiscipline of this kind cannot be regarded in the same way as trade disputes and must be dealt with firmly although not vindictively. Of the demands of the men, that for improvement in quality of the food was met as it was made known, although the standard of rations in this service is already above the Army.*

Sri M Annathasayanam Ayyangar:- Wretched quality.

Mr P Mason: I have seen the food.

Sri M Annathasayanam Ayyangar:- Did you take the food?

Mr President: - Order, Order, Let the member finish.

Mr P Mason: *Of other demands, those relating to individual officers and men are being inquired into.* **No one has yet heard what it is that Commander King is supposed to have said. He himself is quite definite that he used no insulting language.** *The question is, however, being enquired into. Nor is it known in Delhi what was the charge against RK Singh. Tel Dutt was dismissed from service for writing slogans on HMIS Talwar. This is simple disciplinary action and no service can proceed if the acts of Commanding Officers are to be called in question by ratings. Of the remaining demands which appear to be most important relate to rates of pay and gratuity. As I have already explained in connection with RIAF the rates of pay in this service as in the Air Force are considerably higher than in the Indian Army. If you raise the pay of the Navy you would certainly have to raise the pay of the Army with inevitable repercussions on the wage level throughout the country. I put it to the* *house that it is at present impossible for India's finances to accept the proposal that the wages of Indian servicemen should be raised to the level of British service which are related to wage levels in the United Kingdom. If such a demand is to be accepted, it would mean that the size of the armed forces would have to be considerably reduced.*

In the light of this general statement, I turn to the detailed question. Before that I would like to give some more recent news which has come in the morning.

Seth Yusuf Haroon Abdoola : *the honourable member has not referred to Karachi.*

Mr Mason : *I am going to do that. Here is report received from Karachi this morning. Himalya which is Gunnery School, Chamak that is the Radar school, and Bahadur which is one of the two Boys Training establishments, and all the three of which are on Manora Island are quiet although they are affected. It remains to be seen if they return to their duties this morning. They were addressed last night and received the address of their Commanding Officer in a reasonable spirit. The sloop Hindustan is in the hands of mutineers. It has personnel of about 300 ratings, The position regarding this ship was that yesterday a number of ratings from shore establishments tried to reach the ship. They reached the ship and my statement, that is slightly different from that to the press—but I am not quite sure which is right, as I have not had my information confirmed, but my information is that the military police went to the ship to arrest those who had left the shore Establishments to go to the ship and they were fired on from the ship. They then returned the fire of the ship and thereupon HMIS Hindustan opened fire with all her guns. The firing lasted about ten minutes. This morning HMIS Hindustan is berthed alongside and Commodore Curtis, who is Naval Officer in Charge, is going to the ship this morning in a final attempt to make them see reason. If they do not force will have to be used. The shore establishment Dilawar, another Boys Training establishment at Karachi, which is on the main-land is unaffected. Another shore Establishment, the Torpedo School, is also unaffected. All small arms and ammunition have been removed from Manora establishments and it is expected that these establishments would return to duty today. Commodore Curtis spoke to them last night and he received what is described as an Ovation. That is the position in Karachi.*

The last news from Bombay is that by 8 o'clock last night all available small arms and ammunition at Castle Barracks were surrendered to the Naval Officers who entered the barracks. The ratings in the dockyard and ships still have arms. There was much talk between the ships by signal during the night. This is a point to which I would draw the particular attention of the house. It appeared from these radio signals between ships that there are two parties among them. Majority of the mutineers were impressed by the warning given to them by the Flag Officer Commanding the Royal

Indian Navy and by the Flag Officer Bombay and would like today to come to terms. There is, however, a small party who advocate continued violence. They say that the support of all the political parties is behind them, therefore, they would proceed in their attempt. They say the case is going to be discussed in what they refer to as parliament, which I think may mean the Assembly.

There was little rioting in the city during the night, which, I do not think arose out of the disturbances as it does not appear that the ratings were taking part in it. I think that goondas of the city were taking part in it. One sub Lieutenant of RNVR was killed by a bullet. There was no wide spread disturbance at Bombay and the ships were flying 'cease fire' flag. In all the shore establishments the situation is that the majority of men in the establishment are quiet but is refusing to work.

Karachi, I have given you the position. At Jamnagar, Valsura, Torpedo School is unaffected. Cochin is unaffected. Madras- 80 ratings marched through the streets in sympathy with the Bombay men but returned quietly to their barracks on the advice of their officer. Vizagapatam- The position is same as in Madras. 150 ratings demonstrated but returned quietly. Calcutta- 400 ratings still refuse to work. In Delhi, My friend asked, 39 men yesterday refused duty and were arrested. This is the news I have.

Perhaps it would help the house if I read out the whole question part by part and repeat the answer.

Question 72 (a) When did the strike start? This has been answered. (b) Whether Government made any inquiry and (c) whether Government is contemplating appointing any Inquiry Committee?

Answer to (b) and (c) –

The first is for the men to return to duty. When this is done full inquiry will be held.

(d) Whether it is a fact that the strike was due to some of the ratings being arrested?

(e) Whether it is a fact that these arrests followed because of the trainees shouting political slogans and INA slogans? Answer – One of the causes alleged by the men, though I should say I do not believe it, is the punishment of two men. RK Singh and Dutt, but this does not appear to be the main cause.

(f)- Whether it is a fact that they were harshly treated and given severe punishment .

(g) and the action Government contemplate taking, (h) whether the strike was due because of rigorous punishment awarded to some of the ratings, (I) Whether it is a fact that the officer in charge was unduly and unjustly rude to them and (j) what

action the Government contemplates taking against the officers in question.—The answer to all these points is that the information is not available at present but the matter will be inquired into fully as the ratings return to work.

Question 74, (a) the date on which the ratings struck work, (b) whether the cause of their action was the insulting and abusive language used by Commander King, (c) whether on and after 18th instant the ratings in the other Units and establishments ceased work—I have answered that.

(d) Whether ratings of the ships at sea have also joined in the strike. Answer—No Sir, as far as I know none. (e) Whether the number of strikers now exceeds 15000. Answer—It is rather less than 12000. (f) Whether all the strikers have jointly set up a Central Naval Strike Committee. Answer—Yes Sir. (g) and (h) refer to grievances, which I explained at length. (h) asks what measures the Government has taken, to that the answer is that the full inquiry will be made as soon as the men have returned to work.

Mr MR Masani (Bombay City Urban): *Will the honourable member kindly state if it is a fact that, as reported in the Free Press Journal of Bombay, of February 19, the language used by Commander King to his ratings included phrases like "Sons of coolies" and "Sons of bitches"*

Mr P Mason: *I have not seen that report but as I said, the question what he said will be inquired into and is being inquired into and he himself is quite positive that he used no insulting language.*

ROLL OF HONOUR

The sailors were all alone in their struggle against the naval injustice and the junior sailors were in the forefront. On 19 March 1946, the PRO, GHQs in its press communiqué released the list of ratings killed or injured in Bombay on 21 February and in Karachi on 22 February 1946 during the mutiny.

At Bombay,

Death : Krishnan, Leading Sick Berth Attendant

Injured : 1- M. Azad, PO; 2- PC Acharaya, Leading Stoker; 3- Mohd. Ali, Stoker; 4- U. Hayat, Stoker 11; 5- NA Shah, Able seaman; 6- G Shah Seaman Boy.
One officer Sub/Lieutenant Cowell was killed in civil rioting.

Exhaustive checks were made and 32 ratings could not be accounted for. They were presumed to be deserters.

At Karachi

Deaths : 1- MN Sainani, Ordinary seaman; 2- Ali Mohd, Ordinary seaman; 3- M Sarwar, Able seaman; 4-Varki, Able seaman; 5- Mohd Rafiq, Boy; 6- Bhattacharya, Boy, 7- Issac, Boy and 8- Mohd Hussain, Able seaman.

Injured : 1- Mohd Ismail, P O; 2- B Singh, Ordinary Seaman; 3- Irzam Singh, Able seaman; 4- J.Singh, Able seaman; 5- G S Khan, Ldg. Seaman; 6- Tara Chand, Able seaman; 7-Abdul Majid, Able seaman; 8- Fazal Haque, Able seaman; 9- S Singh, Able seaman; 10-K Devakaran, Able Seaman; 11- C Lall, Able Seaman; 12- J B Singh, Boy; 13- Ghulam Samdani, Boy1; 14- S Mukerji, Boy1; 15- S Singh, Leading Stoker; 16- F Rehman, Cook; 17- BA Paul, Boy; 18- MA Khan, Boy; 19- M Lewis, Able Seaman; 20- Noor Mohd, Boy 1; 21- Basthan Khan, Boy 1; 22- Ahmed Iqbal, Boy1; 24-Alfred, Boy; 25- N Singh, Able seaman; 26- V Mhadrvan, Stoker 11; 27- Bhacca Said, Cook(S); 28- PK Dutt, Able seaman; 29 - IH Khan, Able seaman; 30- Gurmurthi, Topass; 31- KK Hussain

Khoja, Stoker 1; 32- MK Yasin, Leading Steward;
33- HS Kutty, Leading seaman; 34- S Singh, Telegraphist;
35- Nethianad, Ord. Sig; 36- Mohd Nawaz, Ord.
Sig; 37- Mir Abdul, PO; 38- Mohd Afzal, Able seaman;
39- N Ahmed, Cinema Operator and 40- Hussain, Civilian.

One sailor was found missing and could not be accounted for.

The number and the nature of the casualties clearly shows that 22 February 1946 was the bloodiest and the most ghastly day of the mutiny at Karachi as compared to Bombay where the discontentment among sailors was noticeable since the Navy day on 1 December 1945 at HMIS *Talwar*. Since then, the witch hunt had started and it took toll on these men in the navy.

12

Hidden Truth

Victory celebration was perhaps the only joyous occasion for the Royal Indian Navy after World War II. The uncertain future and bad service conditions cast gloom on the sailors. Bad food, large scale demobilization and non-payment of release benefits added more misery to the naval life. Amidst these depressing conditions, some surreptitious slogans were found written at HMIS *Talwar*. The ensuing change of the Commanding Officer muddled it further with the alleged foul language against the sailors that ultimately resulted in a full blown mutiny by the sailors. The Naval command was transferred to the Commander-in-Chief of India by the Flag Officer Commanding Royal Indian Navy. The senior sailors did not join the mutiny and later the officers were also withdrawn from the naval ships and establishments. The ships generally 'de-ammunition' before berthing in the harbour and the junior sailors could neither sail the ships nor operate gunnery systems independently on board ships. Safety firing arcs fitted on gun mountings restricted the firing of guns in the harbours. This was the nature and degree of threat from the sailors and the Flag Officer commanding the Royal Indian Navy had requisitioned a large number of battle-ready war ships from the fleet of Commander-in-Chief, East Indies to counter it. The Royal Air Force war planes flew low sorties overhead. The highest British military authority in India armed with a battle-ready land, sea and air force was ranged against the directionless, mutinous junior naval sailors in the naval establishments and on board ships in the Bombay harbour. The naval mutiny of the junior sailors was like a repeat of history of the INA that also faced British land, sea, and air forces during the war except that the sailors were in no position to fight this onslaught.

It is a well-known and accepted fact that the victor inevitably scripts the history as he desires. The views of the vanquished are always denounced and depreciated. Even his pleas and forbearance for justice are maliciously thrown overboard. In such a highly biased administrative system, official actions are always deemed to be right and stand justified. In these subjective circumstances even, praises often get showered on men who hardly deserve or not even connected with it. Normally, all the actions and information regarding these events are made classified. It is either heavily censored or suppressed but nature has its own way of unmasking the truth and it gets unravelled in the most innocuous manner.

Defence Organizations are sticklers for rules and regulations. The details of policy and planning for all the armed actions are appropriately classified and are strictly restricted to a need to know basis only. For action against the mutinous naval personnel, a formidable naval task force of several war ships was requisitioned against mutinous junior naval sailors who had no ability to man the guns or fight a sea battle. It was perhaps a highly disproportionate Sea Force that was assembled for action against revolting junior sailors. The aim of this administrative action could perhaps be to immediately snuff out their revolt to help restore order in the naval service. Obviously the details of this classified operation would be known only to those personnel who were specifically and specially chosen for this operation. It is a fact that the Commanding Officer of HMIS *Glasgow*, Captain Hubback, the task force commander, was profusely praised for his splendid cooperation in this naval action against the mutinous sailors in Bombay but he only arrived after the mutiny had ended. This bizarre incident of tailoring the truth was the need of the naval administration.

It was a fact that after handing over the command, the navy was not under control and was only complying with the tasks assigned to it by the Army. It did not have much say in the operations against mutinous sailors after the army action had started on Thursday, 21 February 1946. First, the sailors were ordered to return to the barracks whilst all the civilians and officers had also abandoned their places of duty ashore and afloat. The possibility of sea battle, though extremely remote, would also have been foreseen. The ships under the naval sailors were berthed in the get out and inner harbour or tied along at the breakwater. These were thus completely stranded and would not get any dockyard help to get out and proceed to the sea. The ships from the East Indies Fleet were to assemble at the mouth of the Bombay harbour. Since it was expected that there would not be any requirement for the movement of ships in the harbour, the senior naval officer in charge of Bombay harbour was also called ashore and relieved from the harbour duties.

In such striking and scary army controlled conditions in the Bombay harbour, HMS *Nith*, a Royal Naval Ship, with no role in these operations against the sailors but just en route to the UK from Singapore entered the Bombay harbour on the evening of 21 February 1946. Captain Ian Scott of the Royal Navy was taking passage to the UK on board this ship. As per the naval convention, the entering ship asks for a berth in the harbour but there was no naval authority to allot a berth to his ship. Whilst entering the harbour, HMS *Nith* met two small British ships, a frigate, HMS *Trent* and a Fleet Minesweeper HMS *Mary Rose* at the mouth of the harbour. These ships had been ordered to move out to the sea in view of army action in the Bombay harbour. In such odd and confusing conditions, Captain Scott on board HMS *Nith* came to know about the mutinous conditions in Bombay through voice communication with the two RN ships ordered to proceed to the sea. HMS *Nith* also intercepted some wireless communication pertaining to the unrest in the Royal Indian Navy whilst sailing along the Indian coast en route to Bombay harbour. Quickly taking stock of the situation in the Bombay harbour, Captain Ian Scott found himself to be the senior-most Naval Officer afloat. The appointment of a senior officer afloat is a symbol of order in precedence and to ensure discipline in the harbour. Being the senior officer afloat, he then hoisted the senior Naval Officer afloat burgee on the main mast of HMS *Nith* in accordance with the naval practice and assumed command in the harbour. HMS *Glasgow* came to Bombay on 23 February 1946 after the unconditional surrender of the ratings. It was then that Captain Scott handed over charge of the Senior Naval Officer afloat to Captain Hubback Commanding Officer of HMS *Glasgow*. HMS *Nith* left Bombay on Monday, 25 February 1946.

After reaching England, Captain Ian Scott wrote a detailed account of his activities during his stay in Bombay and titled it as **'BOMBAY WEEKEND'**. He wanted this article to be published in Blackwood, a widely read magazine, and sent the article to the Royal Naval authorities in the United Kingdom (UK) by last week of March 1946 for clearance. The Admiralty forwarded this article to the Royal Indian Naval Liaison Officer in London for his comments. He forwarded the article to the Director of Naval Intelligence in the Admiralty, advising him to suppress its publication. A copy of this article with the recommendatory letter was also sent to Vice Admiral Godffrey Miles, Flag Officer Commanding Royal Indian Navy at the Naval HQs, Delhi. This article describes the ground realities at Bombay and gives a vivid account of a very important phase of this mutiny in the Bombay harbour during 21-25 Feb 1946, the period of his stay in Bombay harbour. Uncensored and relevant excerpts of this article are appended in the succeeding paragraphs.

Bombay Weekend

By Ian Scott

Homeward Bound! There was a feeling of elation, light heartedness aboard, for we were routed to the UK.

As the French took our areas in Indo-China, British and Indian troops were freed to relieve the Australians in Borneo and the outer islands. Boxing Day saw us sail for Labuan, Jesselton and Kuching where we duly relieved the Aussies and concentrated them at Labuan to await early repatriation. Back again, we steamed to Saigon for another Brigade, making both journeys in a sea of strength eight and on the beam at that. It was no way to spend the end of the year but we felt that with the job completed, we might hope to be sailed to home.

At Macassar, a shadow of its peacetime self, we received the welcome news that HMS *Nith* on return to Singapore will be enrouted to the UK. It was just in time, for we were further and further from home and I quite expected to finish up in Sydney in a few weeks' time. Making certain that the 80th Indian Brigade was comfortably settled in their new area and that the liaison with the Dutch Navy was a going concern, we headed west. Ahead of us now would be many days of steaming through empty seas and we decided to get in as much sun bathing as possible before the chill of the Mediterranean forced us into our almost forgotten blue uniform.

At Singapore we were held up for a few days with a broken air pump and those unfortunate members of crew, the regular navy and the others whose age and service groups were in the higher figures, were sent ashore and their place taken by those due for demobilisation. Among the latter were eighty Royal Naval Marines.

Singapore is no place to undertake one's farewell shopping as the prices are still ridiculously high. A cigarette cost six pence, and although the shops are stocked with beautiful stuff, their cost was prohibitory. We were rather glad that we were calling at Bombay where one can obtain almost anything at a reasonable price.

We passed up the Malacca strait, passed our last D Day landing place at Morrib beaches, up past Penang, till Achin Head faded a pale blue blur in our wake. For the fifth consecutive time, I arrived in Colombo on a Sunday, and as the naval staff was in the process of flitting to Trincomalee, we could do little with fuel, water and proceed.

Up the Malabar Coast, we sailed in the calm blue seas, the land a faint hazy line eastwards, with the white fin of dhow sail or the smoke of the distant coaster here and there. Past Cochin, past Goa, and now we were rapidly approaching our furthest north in the last six months. In spite of a blasting sun, it was noticeably cooler.

Over the wireless, we were getting some garbled reports of trouble in Bombay. As I have never been in Bombay when it has been free from trouble, I did not pay attention. True, it appeared to be in trouble this time with the Royal Indian Navy but that was purely political.

We continued our sunbathing and made out our final shopping list for we would get in on Thursday evening and have the weekend in which to complete our purchases. I had mapped out a rather good weekend and was looking forward to it.

At last, we reached Bombay in the late afternoon sunshine. The big blocks of flats on the Marina, the red and white houses climbing the Malabar hill looked so peaceful and quiet. We angled in for the lighthouse and the harbour entrance.

We could see two small war ships coming out, a Frigate and a fleet Minesweeper, and asked their pennants. They were the HMS *Trent* and HMS *Mary Rose,* both British. Where bound? 'We have orders to proceed forth clear of the harbour as the Indian Navy has mutinied and are liable to open fire on you.'

All our ammunition was stowed down in the magazine, ready for arrival in England, and some of the oerilikons were dismantled. Again, we had lost over half the ships' company, and the gun crew now would have to be completed from the passengers. **We set about the business right away. Attempt to call up signal Station and signal Tower failed to produce an answer. HMS *Trent* and HMS *Mary Rose* circled and followed. We let them close and by loud hailer asked them for the latest news.**

We gathered from the confusion coming over the air that things were rather upside down. There was fighting and rioting ashore but the RIN was driven off the streets and now only held their ships, the barracks, the dockyard and two signal stations. There was no contact with the Admiral ashore either by wireless or visual signals. Indeed the trouble had started in the Signal School.

HMS *Mary Rose* had been anchored alongside powerfully armed HMIS *Narbada* while firing was actually going on between the ships and the shore. "Bang goes my blasted Chinese dhow," I said to Grinham. I could see all the craft of the Indian Navy anchored close to the dockyard and the Gateway of India. The largest vessel, the HMIS *Narbada* had her three twin turrets trained on the beach and we heard that all of them had been having a go with the machine guns and rifles at any target which presented itself on the bund. There were some twenty crafts, comprising of destroyers, frigates, sweepers, corvettes and armed yachts, all at anchor.

Our three little ships were heavily outnumbered, outgunned and outranged, but I was damned if we were going to leave harbour. Anyway I had received no signal to that effect and did not intend to. A shout from Grinham and he was only cursing the Marines whom he had trained on HMIS *Narbada* and were eagerly manning the Bofors. We did not want to start a fight when our ammunition was still below and we were well out of our gun range.

The RIN ships, we could see, had hauled down their white ensigns and lay quietly in their berths. No sound broke the stillness of the evening but we already were intercepting their communication from ship to ship on the radio- telephone. One from *Jumna* to *Narbada* made me think, although it was rather pathetic. **"Have no ammunition on board. What are we to do when told to open fire".**

We had closed the range gradually, to about 3000 yards, within an easy range of their guns but still too far to do any damage with HMS *Nith's* light armament, for HMS *Nith*, like HMS *Waveney*, had been fitted as a Headquarter ship and had sacrificed her main armament for extra cabins and offices. All we had were light anti-aircraft guns and mobility.

The present situation had changed all that. **I was now the senior officer afloat, and as there was no contact with the Admiral or the HQ of the Indian Navy, I considered that I had to take charge and deal with the situation as best as I could.** For all I knew, the mutineers might interfere with the commercial dockyards or the immense amount of shipping in the harbour, if the dockyards were covered by the military ashore. **I had to get**

close to the RIN to such a range that we could blast them with our short range guns. Their ships, I noticed, were closed for action and in spite of the heat, no awnings were shipped.

There were two ways I could get close. Firstly, I could steam alongside the HMIS *Narbada* and board with my Royal Marines or I could make an approach by guile and take them without warning. I felt that if we could take the ring leader, the mutiny would collapse but I must know more about the circumstances. **I dropped the anchor, hoisted the senior officer's burgee, and called the meeting of the Commanding Officers.**

HMS *Trent* and HMS *Mary Rose* came over and were joined later by the captain of *Sea belle,* an armed yacht which had just arrived. The latter owned a welcome four inch gun and multiple pom-poms.

Now, I heard that this mutiny had been working up for some time as the ratings had some well-established grievances. These had been submitted in the normal way, but covering as they did a vast scope, nothing had been decided and the ratings had been given no clear indications that their grievances were to be investigated . They complained of food, (a poor quality cooking fat had been provided by the contractors), pay, travelling conditions, the slow demobilization, lack of marriage allowance, lack of re-establishment and their general treatment.

There were plenty of grounds here for bitterness and with a strong additional pressure brought to bear by the political sources, the ratings decided on a non-violent sit down strike. It shows how badly advised they must have been to think that such a thing was possible.

The Strike Committee could not control their men and soon ashore early in the week, the men were parading improperly dressed and shouting insults at any European. Several were manhandled. The Bombay hooligans thought this was too good an opportunity to miss and they joined in with their usual violence. The police and the military were called to round up and incarcerate the mutineers. They were stoned, assaulted, and knifed. Cars of all kinds and army lorries were ambushed, stoned and set on fire. Firing occurred on both sides and the casualties mounted. The mutineers driven into the dockyard and barracks, defended themselves with rifles and machine guns, but the rioting and looting became more widespread as the mill hands and students joined the melee. Young men, well dressed, could be seen at many corners waiting to stone any car or bus stupid enough to proceed unescorted. Violent crowds looted wine shops, clothing stores and food shops and attacked any foreign shop and any bank. Isolated people were robbed and murdered.

Such was the picture of Bombay on my arrival. It was a beautiful calm evening, the end of a lovely day. I had my small force bunched and ready. **We remained where we were, guns ready and double sentries posted, while I reported the situation to the C-in-C East Indies, for I was uncertain if the Admiral ashore was in touch with him.**

That he was, I discovered very quickly, for every warship within miles was now ordered to proceed to Bombay at full speed (a cruiser, two destroyers and six frigates). Two frigates will arrive in the next twelve hours. I was ordered on no account to attack unless I was heavily attacked by mutineers.

We decided on a single plan. I would fuel at the first light and be followed by the others in single order. **I would then close HMIS *Narbada* on the excuse of discussing matters with them, and the ships would come one at a time anchoring in most strategic positions for close range action. The night passed quietly, except on the radio telephones which hummed with rather childish signals.**

"Don't get excited by firing, this is mostly dummy, so keep non-violent system"

"Water for drinking and cooking purpose only. We may not be able to get water for some time."

"Be patient boys, we are sure to achieve our strike."

"There are rumours that at the silent hours of the night, troops will come alongside fully equipped and take control. Men might be taken ashore under escort. It is requested that all personnel maintain complete non-violence and be calm and disciplined."

On the way to fuel I signalled '*Narbada*', "Can you come over and discuss matters with me this morning? I will close you and anchor after fuelling." The casual signal I thought covers our approach without causing them to panic or take rash action. I must admit that I expected the ringleader himself on board my ship, and I did not expect an answer. All I wanted was an excuse to get close.

Surprisingly I received an answer about an hour later. **"We have no executive officer on board (I knew all officers had been put shore) but if you wish to come on board us do so."** I will admit swift thoughts of a bullet, of a knife, or at least being held hostage passed through my mind, but this was an opportunity too good to miss. The motor boat was called away, and taking one officer with me, Lieutenant Commander Bacon RNVR, we were soon approaching *Narbada*.

We had intercepted messages during the night that the Indian Army and Indian Air Force had joined the mutineers but this was just wishful thinking on their part. **I also knew that they were getting short of food and water, so I had every hope that they would listen to what I had to say.**

The ship's company of *Narbada* lounged around the decks without caps and not looking friendly at all but I could see no sign of weapons. I was greeted on the quarter deck by a polite but cap less petty officer who asked me to come up to the captain's cabin. I noticed en route that the wardroom was empty and the ship fairly clean.

There was some delay and the doctor of the ship came to tell us that a conference was in session consisting of a member from every ship in the harbour under the President of the Strike Committee. This was all to the good, I thought, and would save us from a lot of trouble.

At last I turned the handle and walked in to find some fifty Indians seated in rows. I wished them 'Good morning' to which they all replied 'Good morning, Sir'. I told them I just arrived from the Far East and was not in touch with their grievances and that I would like them to explain. They were of different shades, races and religious denominations, but all looked to me to be good and intelligent. They all tried to talk at once but soon I had them telling me all about it, politely and clearly.

I asked them if they had forwarded their grievances in the correct manner and how long ago had they done so. **They protested that they were not responsible for the bad behaviour of the few ashore and were completely non-violent.** I told them that they would undoubtedly be held responsible for all the trouble ashore which would not have happened without their rash mutiny. "You know as well as I do that the riffraff ashore only wait for such an excuse. You should have thought of that before. Another thing, it is not good to call this a strike, it is a mutiny."

"You have made your grievances clear to the entire world and in doing so you have been the cause of many casualties to your own countrymen. **There is absolutely no reason why this should go on. You can gain only a more severe punishment. On the other hand, a graceful surrender now only can do well and it is much more dignified than being blown out of water or being taken ashore in irons. You cannot argue with eight cruisers.**"

One delegate got to his feet. "Sir", he said, "We must go on for we have not achieved a single point yet. We are prepared for prison or death in the cause of our shipmates." "That line is of no value," I told him there had never been a mutiny in the navy when they were granted a single concession while the mutiny continued. **I can assure you quite honestly that the sooner you call it off, the better it will be to all and for the attainment of your demands.** You look like intelligent men. Surely you can see that I am giving you a very sound advice".

They were obviously affected with this simple reasoning and again hastened to assure me that all the guns were trained fore and aft, all the ammunition below, and all the small arms locked up. "You haven't much time" I **told them, "War ships are speeding here and with them may come another senior naval officer of a different type who may shell you first and then talk to you afterwards. Hoist your white ensign again and recall your officers on board."**

It was then that I discovered the mutiny was actually run from the shore for they told me that they must first consult with the leaders ashore. They seemed a bit perturbed and began discussing the idea with each other.

"You can take it from me," I went on, "**that all your grievances will be properly aired and the action on them at the earliest opportunity.** But do not expect any early demobilization. There are millions of men all over the world in the same state as you are and you at least are in your own country. **I am going ashore to see the Admiral now and will tell him that you are going to be sensible and I hope you will surrender gracefully.** Don't forget that I am on my way home and you are holding me up here."

They laughed and crowded around me. "Can I ask you a question?" a Sikh demanded. "Go ahead," I replied. "Why did you think that *Narbada* was the leading ship?" "Easy," I told him, "*Narbada* was making all the signals." "Did you read them?" I was asked. "Of course", I said, "and very interesting too." They grinned feebly at each other.

Before I left, I saw a signal made out and ready to send, "All ships are to surrender to their own Indian Officers when they come aboard". I asked if they were in touch with their officers and they told they were but did not really expect them to come off without the orders from the Admiral.

I discovered that I had spent a whole hour with them and although I told the Captain of *Nith*, Lieutenant Commander Grinham RNVR that I would come straight back. He seemed rather doubtful that I would get back. **I decided to see the Admiral right away.**

We landed at Ballard Pier which was held by a small detachment of white troops but the large building and clock tower were in the hands of the rebels. However, everything was peaceful. So, borrowing a break we made for the RIN Headquarters. Here, behind the shut gates were the armed Marines as a battle was supposed to be raging in the vicinity. Actually the streets were empty except for a few usual brickbats and coping stones that the Indians so delight in throwing. I never heard a shot.

I made my report to the Admiral, wondering at the time why no signal or officer was sent out to me since my arrival in the harbour for I could think of no good reason to prevent it.

I think the people ashore received a wrong impression of the behaviour of the fleet from the really serious trouble ashore. It seemed a pity to me that no officer went off just as casually as I had done to talk things over with them. Undoubtedly, the C-in-C, East Indies was given a false impression as all the ships were told to enter the harbour at the action stations and all the ship companies hoped that they were in for a scrap.

When I landed, I met an Indian officer who asked permission to broadcast from Nith, a threat of overwhelming strength and demand for an unconditional surrender. I told him to wait until I saw the Admiral as I thought it might have the wrong effect after my talk to the delegates.

I talked to the GOC, General Lockhart, over the telephone giving him my impressions, and suggesting that a return of all officers would probably see the end of the business.

The Admiral insisted on his broadcast so it was put over the radio telephone and also by the loud hailer from a boat which went from ship to ship. They were told they were up against the overwhelming forces both afloat and ashore, that the Air Force would fly over them and any attempt to fire would be answered by bombs. The sign of total surrender was to be the masthead hoisting of a large blue or black flag.

As the frigates began to arrive, I anchored them around the rebel fleet and soon large notices appeared, 'Non Violence – Do not shoot'.

In the afternoon, all the ships hoisted their white ensigns to half-mast. I learnt afterwards that as a sign they would comply with my suggestions and as a mark of respect for those killed ashore.

Through the night of Friday-Saturday, a rowdy argument went on between the President of the Strike Committee afloat and his opposite number ashore. One from afloat read 'Surrender gracefully'. I seemed to recognize that. Another one read, 'Surrender gracefully – carry on strike'. The answer naturally enough was, 'Do not understand message'. Then, 'Do not surrender gracefully. Be peaceful and keep on striking come what may. Let anything happen'. This was of course from the beach.

The mutiny was over

At 0755 hrs, *Narbada* hoisted the preparative, a clear sign that they resumed naval procedures and at 0800 hrs, all colours were hoisted close up. **Immediately, I sent off two officers to take control of *Narbada*, signalling C-in-C that the mutiny was over. I went ashore to make certain that the RIN officers should go on board but found that it had been done already, and it was decided to take sixty percent of each crew ashore on Sunday when armed guards would be placed abroad.**

British war ships were still arriving one after the other without knowing that the show was over. I received a signal from a pugnacious frigate. "Have thirty six fully armed, ready for boarding or duty ashore." I felt sorry for them as we had felt exactly the same.

On Saturday, late in the forenoon, the skipper of *Narbada* came to see me, a commander in the RIN. He was not very happy about things and knowing that I had eighty Marines on board he asked whether I would be willing to let them guard the four biggest RIN vessels that night. His request was arranged and in addition I placed on board each ship, a British officer, the Captain of the Marines and three Lieutenant Commanders RNVR, all ex CO's who were taking passage to home in Nith.

The Royals, hoping till the end that they might have an excuse for a scrap, went on board cheerfully only to discover that their Indian ship's companies were extremely friendly. They even insisted on the British films being shown as opposed to the Indian ones in honour of their guests,

Everything seemed to be well in hand afloat, although trouble continued ashore. **The *Glasgow* arrived on Saturday evening, I turned over the duties and responsibilities of senior officer afloat to her.** There was little to do now. I allotted them all anchor berths as they arrived, and the ring around the ex-rebels was complete.

This show of swift and efficient power must have made the mutineers realize they had been wise in taking my advice. I went ashore to dine with the Governor, quite satisfied that our job was done.

From the Governor of Bombay, (what a job) I heard more about the scenes ashore. They had a bad time that unfortunately continued but the police and military did a good job. The trouble was dying down. In fact, the trouble seemed far away as we dined in the garden overlooking the light-studded bay below the Malabar hill. The table lit under the moonless canopy of night by the candles stuck amongst the flowers in their bowls. The early curfew appeared unbroken, but it flared up again in the night in the northern outskirts of the city. The Sunday dawned in peace while the army took over the control of the RIN ships at noon and my Marines returned in time for a hot meal. The Sunday night was our last night in Bombay and with the curfew still at 1930 hrs, there was not very much we could do ashore.

Grinham and I however accepted an invitation to an all-Indian club on the bund. This is an attractive little place on the edge of the harbour, with beautifully trimmed lawns beset with gay flowers. Although the club was fairly full, we were the only two white people there, and yet I have never spent a more enjoyable evening in Bombay. That afternoon I was in the almost deserted Bombay yacht club, empty because of the trouble still going on. **In that club, no Indian is allowed as a member or a guest.** It seemed rather significant to me. For I, who had spent many years in foreign countries, **found this intolerance hard to understand and it had undoubtedly played its part in the present situation in India.** I have friends of many nationalities, even Japanese, and I find that when one has the harshest thoughts of their countries and their inhabitants, these thoughts are softened by the memories of their good friends.

In the last thirty odd years, I have been present at four naval mutinies, and each one I think, could have been avoided if there were tolerance and sympathy with their men, and if there were that human and personal understanding which exists between an officer and a man in our own small ships.

Bombay sank below the horizon in our creaming wake and the pale blue ghats faded merging into a cloudless sky. The gateway of the East was closing behind us and ahead over the sea miles, laid England.

Captain Scott, an experienced senior rank Royal Naval officer was visiting Bombay for the first time. Obviously, he was not biased against and had no prejudice or malice against the Indian naval personnel. Before reaching Bombay, during sailing along the Indian coast, he came to know about the unrest of the Indian naval Sailors from wireless and radio intercepts broadcasted on naval channels and the trouble with the Royal Indian Navy that appeared to be political. When he was entering the harbour he met two small RN ships, HMS *Trent* and HMS *Rose Mary*, who were ordered to move out to the sea when preparatory action against the naval mutineers in Bombay began after the Royal Indian Navy command was already transferred to the Army. In such conditions, he spoke to the commanding officers of HMS *Rose Mary* and HMS *Trent* who gave him the background and acquainted him with the ground realities in Bombay harbour. The battle lines were now clearly drawn and action against Indian sailors was already underway. There was no naval authority in the Bombay harbour to allot him an anchoring/berthing site. He himself selected an anchor site. During these evolutions, he hardly perceived any threat to his security or his ship. It was presumably tense but all calm and quiet in the Bombay harbour.

The seasoned sea fox, after discussions and careful planning with his ship's officers, boarded the rebelling bigger and better naval gunship HMIS *Narbada*, then flagship of the Royal Indian Navy. In these tense conditions, he singlehandedly interacted with the leaders of the striking sailors from all the ships afloat and assured them, "You can take it from me that **all your grievances will be properly aired and the action on them will be taken at the earliest opportunity." I am going ashore to see the Admiral now and will tell him that you are going to be sensible, and, I hope, you will surrender gracefully.** Light banter followed and before Captain Scott left the ship, he saw the signal ready to be sent out and it read, *"All ships are* *to surrender to their own Indian Officers when they come aboard."* Captain Scott was also invited and complimented by the Governor of Bombay for doing a good job.

It was at first clearly an unmistakable sign that the sailors did not want to fight but were contented that their grievances would be conveyed to the Admiral. Quite contrary to this service like approach, and in spite of known bad morale and security reports concerning HMIS *Talwar*, the very first trouble spot in the chain of events, no such assurance came from its Commanding Officer, Commander King but over the period he created more tension by being highhanded and allegedly using abusive language. For the first time, this assurance came from the Flag Officer Bombay, Admiral Rattrey only at 1700 hrs on 18 February 1946 when sailors in HMIS *Talwar* were already on strike and the other sailors ashore were joining this strike. By this time, the policy of handing over the Navy to the Army authorities and to take stringent action against the sailors was already decided. Captain Scott was not aware of this background when he entered the harbour. However, the Naval and the Army authorities now fully knew from highly reliable source, Captain Scott that the sailors on all the ships in the harbour were willing to surrender even before the ultimatum to surrender unconditionally was broadcasted on the radio by FOCRIN. Evidently, the threat of the naval sailors was overblown and the huge naval task force was requisitioned from the Commander-in-Chief, East Indies. Captain Scott described this gaffe as, **"I think the people ashore had received a wrong impression of the behaviour of the fleet from the really serious trouble ashore. It seemed a pity to me that no officer went off just as casually as I had done to talk things over with them. Undoubtedly the C-in-C, East Indies was given a false impression that all the ships were told to enter the harbour at action stations, and all ship companies hoped that they were in for a scrap."**

Why the above approach could not be taken by the naval authorities is a matter of conjecture. It is likely that the policy was already cast and Captain Scott was not aware of it. He, however, wrote about it in these words, "Over the wireless we were getting some garbled reports of trouble in Bombay. As I have never been to Bombay when it was free from trouble, I did not pay attention. **True, this time it appeared to be in trouble with the Royal Indian Navy but that was purely political."** These political exigencies could only be best known to the Government or those who indulged in these political activities. But surely, one thing was certain that under the then prevailing conditions in India, publication of Captain Scott article would have embarrassed the British Government. It is a fact that the article of Captain Ian Scott was not cleared for publication as requested by him.

Homeward bound after war duties, Captain Ian Scott could not have imagined that fate destined him a role to perform during the mutiny of the sailors at Bombay when his ship *Nith* entered the harbour. Finding no naval authority to allot a berth to his ship, he assumed the duties of senior naval officer in the Bombay harbour. The sailors in the communication departments and the Release Centre were already on hunger strike and other sailors in shore establishments were openly supporting it. The sailors on board ships in the Bombay harbour gathered on the senior naval ship *Narbada* to join the strike when Captain Ian Scott went there. After interaction with the sailors, he saw the draft signal of their surrender also. After that, he interacted with the highest authorities in Bombay including the Governor of Bombay. He told the GOC General Lockhart over the telephone suggesting to him that **"a return of all officers would probably see the end of the business."** But it evoked no action.

The sailors surrendered unconditionally. Captain Scott sent two officers to take control of the Indian naval flag ship HMIS *Narbada* and sent a signal to the C-in-C that the mutiny was over. British war ships were still arriving one after the other without knowing that the mutiny was already over. Everything was well in hand afloat, although trouble continued ashore. **The Glasgow arrived on Saturday evening, and Captain Scott handed over the duties and responsibilities of the senior officer afloat to its Commanding Officer Captain Hubback.** The ring around the mutinous sailor-rebels was complete, as planned.

It is noteworthy to know that the strong fleet requisitioned from C-in-C, East Indies far exceeded the threat of any mutinous sea action. The rebellious sailors were easily subdued by the local military units. The massive show of the British military might have some other considerations as well. This was not a topic for the Inquiry Commission and even Captain Ian Scott who officiated as senior naval officer afloat in Bombay during the mutiny was also not called for by any Board of Inquiry or an Inquiry Commission set up by the Government of India. His article was also not allowed to be published. The contents of his article were also discussed with the British political secretary.

Captain Scott had a ring-side view of the RIN mutiny. He wrote his version of the naval mutiny in Bombay and wanted it to be published in the Blackwood Magazine, a well-read magazine in Europe. In accordance with the service rules, he submitted his article to the RN authorities in UK. As the subject of his article pertained to the Royal Indian Navy, so it was sent to the RIN liaison officer, WR Shewring, in London for further action with the Admiralty. On 2 April 1946 RIN LO sent this article to the Admiralty with these remarks **"I find it difficult to believe this nauseating type of self-publicity coupled with the destructive criticism of the Flag Officer of the Royal Navy could have emanated from the pen of a responsible Naval Officer. It is the opinion of the political secretary that its publication at this stage when the tension in India is very acute would be indiscreet. I wonder whether a gentle tip to Blackwood that the Admiralty is not very pleased with the article would have the desired effect. Black wood has worldwide popularity and I am convinced that the publication of this 'tripe' would have a very bad effect."** He also discussed the matter with the Director of Naval Intelligence in London and the publication of this article was suppressed.

RIN LO sent a copy of Captain Scott's article to Vice Admiral Sir Godffrey Miles, the then Flag Officer commanding the Royal Indian Navy. RIN LO described the article as revolting and did his best to get this article suppressed. This was the ignominious end to Captain Scott's article. The British Government and the Royal naval authorities in London went to a great extent to suppress the truth about the mutiny of sailors in Bombay.

13

Verdict Guilty but Historic

Indiscipline in the Navy was mainly due to the bad service conditions and indifferent behaviour of the officers, particularly the British officers. The sailors who fought the war for the British Empire were discontented because their rightful release benefits were not paid to them before their release from the navy. In HMIS *Talwar*, the premier communication establishment, its Commanding Officer allegedly used abusive language and it snowballed into a hunger strike of sailors resulting in a complete breakdown of the administration. The officers and the senior sailors absolved themselves with only the junior sailors carrying the torch of the mutiny and therefore, consigned to be found guilty.

The Officers are the leaders of men and the senior naval sailors are to guide their juniors. This dictum is not only for war conditions but must also be followed in peace time. In war time sailors suffered bad service conditions, slighting behaviour of the officers and a deficient higher command taking these to be war time pressures. But in peace time, the naval authority had also absolved itself of bad administration leading to bad service conditions and depriving sailors of their rightful release dues which led to acts of insubordination by the sailors. The insubordination that took the shape of the mutiny was tried according to the naval law but the failures of the naval administration leading to mutiny and foul mouthing at juniors were wilfully side lined. The ends of justice were not adequately met. There was wide disparity and partiality in the application of naval law. It only took cognisance of indisciplined acts of junior sailors but chose to ignore acts of omission and commission of the Commanding Officer and other higher naval authorities. Removal from command is punishment in the naval terminology and the Commanding Officer of *Talwar*, Commander King, was summarily removed from the command but he was not called for evidence by any Board of Inquiry or an Inquiry Commission. The naval discipline act was not for him. Even adverse entry of his removal from command, if endorsed, in his service dossier appeared to be doubtful. He was first appointed as First Lieutenant and Gunnery Officer of under refit HMS *Achilles* which was commissioned as a flag ship of the Royal Indian Navy after independence. He escaped naval law and was granted regular promotions after being removed from the command of *Talwar* and retired as a Commodore from the Royal Navy. The officers and the senior sailors had kept themselves aloof so that they were not accountable. It was only the junior sailors who were accused for all the ills of naval service that led to mutiny in the navy. Perhaps naval law was subverted to show and punish only junior ratings and absolve all others for their acts of omission or commission leading to mutiny in the service.

The fear of injustice was writ large on their faces when the ratings unconditionally surrendered. They knew about the consequences of waging mutiny whether with or without violence. It was a court martial offence and the punishment could be death. The naval authorities were also feeling guilty of bad administration but had no fear of consequences as their inefficiency was not subject to any investigations. The course of justice was therefore modified accordingly, keeping in view that court martial, being an open court trial was bound to earn more adverse publicity and attached political disadvantage. Even the ring leaders were not tried by court martial but were punished summarily. This course of justice that had already been thought of was also known to Captain Ian Scott before he left Bombay on 24 February 1946. He even knew the manner in which it would be implemented. **He knew that it had been decided to take sixty per cent of each crew ashore on Sunday when armed guards would be placed aboard ships.** These ratings were to be taken to a concentration camp set up at Mulund at Bombay for interrogation. They were awarded summary punishments and discharged from the service without release benefits.

In order to expeditiously deal with the naval personnel after the mutiny, the Flag Officer Commanding the Royal Indian Navy issued instructions to all the naval authorities. Under these instructions, any sailor could be suspected and arrested whether he took any or no part in the mutiny. No evidence was required as a proof of participation in any unlawful activity. Anyone could be placed under arrest. All suspected ring leaders were to be dealt with immediately by summary trials. It further clarified that only the worst cases could be tried by court martial. In these cases, caution was also to be exercised because the charges of capital nature cannot be tried by summary trials. In such cases a lesser charge could be levied in lieu. This order was in fact a blanket clearance. In a nutshell, any sailor suspected to have indulged in acts of violence, whether on or outside a ship or an establishment, or who opened fire in Castle Barracks, ships in Bombay or Karachi, or even suspected to be involved in hooliganism in civil streets, were being ordered to be summarily dealt with immediately. This all-encompassing and oppressive naval policy was further modified and strengthened by the Commander-in-Chief of India. In his order, he even outlined the method to adduce evidence in case it is not readily forthcoming. In such cases a definite order was to be given in front of reliable witnesses to the suspected person to perform a definite task. His refusal clearly would become a fit case for immediate disciplinary action against him. This punitive procedure was to continue until considered necessary and the bulk of men who had been misled, realized their folly of disobedience of the naval command. Such was the degree of inhuman brutality of British authorities to the men who helped them to sail to victory in the World War. Without any compassion, the unjustifiable verdict of guilty was already enunciated and implemented. The procedure for naval justice was a mere formality.

There was no trust between the naval authorities and the sailors. Flag Officer Bombay, Rear Admiral Rattray conveniently forgot his promise of 'no punishment to the representatives of the strike committee' given to the sailors in his last meeting with sailors in HMIS *Talwar* on 18 February 1946. It was well known that the senior sailors were not supporting the strike by the junior sailors. P O (Tel) Madan Singh, a senior sailor, known for his cool and calm nature agreed to become a member of the Strike Committee and represent the grievances of the junior sailors as desired by Flag Officer Bombay. Under the new draconian naval instructions, he had to suffer three and a half months of solitary confinement and dismissal from the service with no opportunity given to defend himself. Earlier L Tel Dutt voiced discontent by writing slogans in HMIS *Talwar*. He was also summarily dealt with and discharged from the service.

The Navy neither improved service conditions during the war nor was it prepared to do so after the war. The long simmering discontentment situation was first allowed to drift into hunger strike by a hand full of sailors and then into a mutiny by all the naval sailors in the navy. The highest military authority also spelt out methods to frame charges against them and wilfully threw the principles of justice to the winds. Only Railway warrants were given to the sailors for journey to their homes. The injustice to them was also felt by their families and these are the findings of the Inquiry Commission set up by the Government of India. This is how the mutiny of sailors was brought under control and the verdict of the guilty was already pronounced without any investigations. The mutiny of sailors tapered off as a bad dream. It brought tears and misery to the sailors who were unceremoniously thrown out of the naval service and also their families.

The inept and highly arrogant attitude of the British naval authorities of not dealing fairly with the legitimate grievances of Indian sailors was typically imperialistic. It was devoid of any intention to listen to their grievances, but to ruthlessly stomp out their complaints of foul and abusive language by their Commanding Officer. In a politically surcharged condition in the country, it provided a handle to the political parties to further their interests and intensify their efforts for the freedom of India. The mutiny of Indian naval sailors was not a political movement yet it helped political parties to pitch harder for the Independence of India. The navy under Commander-in-Chief of India deliberately avoided open trials because the resultant adverse publicity would vitiate an already politically surcharged atmosphere in the country at a time when the British Government was engaged in finding a solution to the Independence for India.

Historic

Bombay, a historical place, is the confluence of culture and politics. Firstly, the demand of Self-Government and later the 'Quit India' movement in August 1942 were launched from Bombay. In early 1946, it became the epicentre of the naval mutiny and the sailors were defying naval authorities due to bad service conditions. Concurrent trials of INA personnel, then in progress, together with the trials of sailors for revolt in the navy would further strengthen the already rising fervour in the country. The trials of INA personnel and mutiny by the sailors were distinctly different, yet both added to Indian nationalism and so were politically important. INA fought an open war against the British under the dynamic and vibrant leadership of Netaji Subash Chandra Bose, once a top National Congress leader, whilst the sailors adopted Gandhi's non-violent hunger strike to confront the British naval authority. Later, some unruly sailors also indulged in some violent actions. The naval mutiny was not politically inspired but it had great political bearing and helped hasten independence though the political parties had remained detached from the mutiny of the sailors.

Both the battles of the INA and the naval mutiny were non-political but nonetheless had potentially high voltage political implications against the British injustice. The best thing was that both movements were not biased due to religion, caste or creed, and were therefore, more popular and appealing to win over the support of the Indian masses. Both movements were also under glaring spotlights and widely covered by the radio, press, both English and Vernacular newspapers. Both movements were highly sensitive to the national cause of freedom to India. They enlivened and doubled the national urge for justice amongst all sections of people all over India irrespective of their religious or political beliefs. These movements unified all Indians and encouraged them to seek nothing less than complete Independence of India. If defeat of the INA in the war had heartened Britain and toughened their attitude regarding the issue of Indian independence, the wave of upsurge generated by the sailors mutiny not only revived but further strengthened the will of the nation for Indian independence among the people of India. All the people in India now stood up for the Independence of India.

The sailors were political novices. True, few sailors were led astray by the political elements but they wielded no political influence in the service. It is indisputable that the main causes of the mutiny in the navy were bad service conditions and foul mouthing against sailors by the British officers. After the war, India was politically alive to wrest independence from Britain and thus any agitation against the British authorities would evoke sympathy in all political quarters. Some political parties helped, whilst some others cautioned restraint to the sailors who participated in the mutiny. It is therefore undeniable that the naval mutiny did have political implications also. This fact was vouched by Captain Scott during his stay in Bombay. He also assessed and described the mutiny by the sailors to be purely political in his article. This article was sent to the British political Secretary for comments and he said "**When the tension in India is very acute, publication of the article by Captain Scott would be indiscreet.**" The mutiny of sailors, a non-political upshot had underscored and voiced against injustice by the British naval authorities. The mutiny of sailors against the British officers showed that Britain did not enjoy their confidence. It was a jolt to British confidence as it helped to revive and rekindle the national spirit against the British injustice. The renewed national verve and vigour now solely aimed at Independence of India. The 1946 mutiny of sailors helped to hasten and wrest independence from the British Crown. It is another matter that emotionally united India politically agreed to partition on religious lines.

After the partition of India, naval assets were divided between India and the newly created Pakistan As per choice, majority of Muslim sailors in erstwhile Royal Indian Navy opted to go to the Royal Pakistan Navy. Both the fledgling navies needed trained naval personnel to man their ships but both refrained to recall the sailors discharged from the service during the 1946 mutiny. British naval hegemony prevailed in both the new born navies. Well after quarter century of the mutiny, the Indian Government made amendments. It granted recognition of 'Freedom Fighters' to all the sailors discharged from the naval service after the mutiny but their compatriots now in Pakistan could not bask in this glory. Indian Navy had also honoured two leaders of 1946 naval mutiny, Petty officer Madan Singh and L Tel BC Dutt by naming two oceans going tugs of Indian Navy after their names. In 2001, the Indian Navy laid a wreath and constructed the RIN Mutiny Memorial at Colaba, Mumbai the birth place of the naval mutiny.

14

Mutiny Revisited

Although a string of mutinies took place in some ships and establishments of RIN during mid-1942, mid-1944 & early 1945, these were short lived and localized cases. The mutineers were isolated, charged for acts of indiscipline, summarily tried and discharged from service. Perhaps war & fear of war time restricted these incidents to be treated as local issues. In comparison to these incidents, the naval mutiny in 1946 was a major event of national importance against the British rule. The ongoing political activities and trials of INA personnel further helped surge political passions. It may not be of much surprise that under these politically charged circumstances, the sailors could be reasonably suspected to be in contact or under the influence of some political elements and thus indulging in subversive activities in the service. It was not only widely expressed, but also a much believed factor by the Royal Indian Naval administration. This could however not be substantiated. Even 'Enquiry Commission' was not able to find any political connection between the sailors and any of the political parties. It is also possible that the sailors were political novices and perhaps could have been led astray. The naval mutiny was not openly supported by any political party, yet it inspired and created such political impact that helped to hasten the independence of India.

After the Second World War ended, the mutiny in the RIN in February 1946 was a challenge that Royal Naval Officers faced. The role of Royal Indian Navy, considered adjunct of Royal Navy of England, needed to be redefined after the war, and also considerably curtailed. Consequently, its strength which was over 20000 men & 2400 officers in December 1945 after the war was limited to approximately 1615 both officers and sailors, as per the pre-war sanctions. It was a delicate task that required a statesman's approach to deal with problems arising there from in a humane manner. It will be appreciated that decision to change the then Royal Indian Marines (RIM) to Royal Indian Navy (RIN) had remained under the consideration of British Government from 1925 to 1934, and it is only after that the Royal Indian Navy was formed. Thereafter, it was manned by Royal Naval officers & Indian sailors. At the beginning of the Second World War, eligible Indians were also inducted as officers into RIN. Indian cadets were trained in the United Kingdom (UK) along with the British cadets. These cadets also did their afloat training as cadets and midshipmen as also carried out watch keeping duties on board Royal Naval Ships. Post-independence in 1947, these Indian officers were of junior rank and could not be appointed for staff duties in the Naval Headquarters (NHQ). One of the cadets from Dufferin, who was selected for commission in RIN in 1938, was just of a Lieutenant rank in1946, when the mutiny took place in the Navy. In 1953, he was appointed as Director, Naval Plans (DNP) at NHQs. Indian navy was then, quite used to looking at Britain for its requirements. Indian Navy wanted to start its 'Submarine' branch. Some apprentices were then sent to the UK for S/M and Fleet Arm Training, but Britain was hesitant and not forthcoming. Consequently, there were notions that the Royal Navy was trying to control the expansion of Indian Navy. It was no surprise to IN officers because Royal Naval officers in NHQ had been already acquiring old and redundant naval ships from England, for induction into the Indian Navy. Much before independence of India, it had even sent Indian Naval crew to England for training & acquisition of first Indian Naval Flag ship HMIS *Delhi*. It was followed by induction of ships as follows.

1948-49	'Rajput', 'Rana', and 'Ranjit' - 11 Destroyer Squadron
1951-52	'Godavari', 'Gomati', and 'Ganga' - 22 Destroyer Squadron
1955-56	'Mysore' Cruiser
1957-58	'Brahamputra', 'Beas', and 'Betwa'
1958-80	'Khukri','Kirpan', and 'Kuthar'

It is noteworthy that since its formation in 1934, and also from 1947 to 1958, the Chief of Naval staff of Indian Navy was from the Royal Navy and guided IN expansion.

In 1939, when the Second World War became imminent, the naval strength was substantially increased to over 21000, but soon after the war it was to be reduced to peace-time sanction in shortest time. This cruel and callous attitude of the naval administration towards its men who fought in the war was very depressing not only for these men but also their families. Their disenchantment with naval administration was spontaneous and very obvious. The naval administration had failed to appreciate implication of this decision. This decision was diametrically opposite to longest time (1925 to 1934) that it took to decide the formation of Royal Indian Navy. Incidentally RIN then was merely a skeletal service for harbor duties.

Victory Celebrations at the end of war, was perhaps the only joyous occasion for Indian Naval sailors. Soon after the war, they were looking at the impending bleak future. It was very demoralizing and it shook their confidence, especially the junior ratings who were not very well-groomed into service discipline. Such elements inadvertently had fallen victim to the vicious propaganda that helped pave the way for subversive activities in the service. The ongoing trials of the INA personnel had also vitiated political passions and the political parties generally sympathized with their cause. It is this type of covert and surreptitious approach that could have promted and emboldened the ratings to defy the naval authorities during 1946 naval mutiny. The ratings afloat, on board ships in Bombay harbour, had adopted Gandhian method of non-cooperation and resorted to passive resistance through hunger strike, whilst the ratings in shore establishments took out processions along with the labour and dockworkers' unions. The sailors ashore also were engaged in small encounters with the army personnel sent by the military authorities to quell the mutiny. It clearly pointed that some elements from political parties believing in violent or nonviolent actions were in contact with the naval ratings. However, their association with the naval ratings could not be conclusively proved. The Congress and the Communist Party of India were the main and active political parties in Bombay in 1946. Some sailors had also approached the Congress leaders to intervene with the naval authorities on their behalf. It could not be ascertained if such a request was also made to any leaders of other political party by the sailors. It is now an accepted fact that the 1946 naval mutiny had politically helped the cause of Independence of India. The Government has, though belatedly, accepted this fact. In 1980, the sailors who rebelled against the British Naval & Military authorities have been awarded the status of Freedom fighters.

The belated recognition of these sailors as freedom-fighters points to a careful approach that seemed to be, having political overtones then prevailing in the country. Obviously, the ratings who offered passive resistance like hunger strike or openly took up arms against British naval authorities could have been infused with the political ideologies of those times. The ultimate goal 'Freedom of the country' was achieved, but what followed it was that the British naval officers' still controlled naval resurrection and directed its growth as a naval service. The observation by first Indian Director of Naval Plan that Indian Navy was then used to only looking at Britain for its requirements was very apt. It correctly summed up British attitude to Indian Naval aspiration. During the same period, Russia was willing to help the Indian navy. By early sixties, Indian Navy lessened its dependence on Royal Navy and started sending its officers and men to Russia for training and acquisition of naval ships and submarines from the Russian Government. It not only involved a different technology, but also impinged on social behaviour of the naval personnel. The social order in Russia was different to that in England and it became a cause of discord between officers and men sent to Russia for training/ acquisition of ships and equipment. In these circumstances, slogans were found written against the officers there. It was followed by a Topass's procession in Bombay, for the reason that like in Russian Navy, the Topass branch in the Indian Navy is also going to be abolished. It was in this scenario of unrest and uncertainty that the celebrations of Silver Jubilee of 1946 Naval Mutiny, and shortly after it, the Silver Jubilee celebrations of the Independence Day, became a cause of concern because it was politically right time also to visit these old memories.

Silver Jubilee of Independence Day was ceremonious, but that of 1946 Naval Mutiny saw great upsurge in the subversive activities of the naval service. Typed leaflets, subversive pamphlets distributed and widely mailed by post to many ships and naval authorities, subversive writing and some acts of hauling down flags/hoisting black flag on naval mast and hunger strike etc., were reported by many ships and naval establishments. The organizers tried to create the spirit of 1946 naval mutiny, but failed in mobilizing naval sailors resorting to open mutiny. One of their pamphlets, addressed as fellow communicators commends the deeds of B C Dutt in 1946 sailors' mutiny and exhorts all communicators against unjust naval practices. (See Annexure III) In course of time, all miscreants indulging in these subversive activities were caught and disciplinary action taken against them, as was done during the 1946 Naval Mutiny.

INWARD TELEGRAM

5
$215

(If in any case the communication of the contents of
this document to any person outside British or U.S.
Govt. Service is authorised, it must be paraphrased).

Allotted to Military Department.
Copies to R.I.N.L.O.
Copies circulated.

CYPHER TELEGRAM

From	Government of India. War Department
To	Secretary of State for India
Dated	New Delhi. 23.20 hours, 20th February 1946
Received	16.30 hours, 21st February 1946

IMPORTANT

No. 1171.   SECRET.

Regret to report serious disciplinary trouble has broken
out in Royal Indian Navy, main facts of which are as follows.

1. On Monday, 18th Feb., all ratings except Chief Petty Officers and
Petty Officers in H.M.I.S. Talwar R.I.N. Signal School, Bombay,
refused duty and to listen to their officers. They shouted
political slogans, particularly at the Commanding Officer. The
establishment comprises approximately 1,100 ratings. Rear
Admiral Rattray the Flag Officer, Bombay, took charge personally
and reports that he considers the affair has political origin.
The disaffected ratings demanded that a political leader be
allowed to address them. This was not permitted. On Tuesday,
19th, the trouble spread to the R.I.N. depot and Castle Barracks
Bombay, and to ship in Bombay Harbour. There has been
considerable rowdyism in the streets and the civil police have
made some arrests of ratings involved in acts of violence. One
incident in which the American flag is alleged to have been torn
down and destroyed by persons in R.I.N. uniform is being
separately reported.

2. The Flag Officer Bombay received 14 delegates from the
mutineers and was presented with a list of demands which include
the following

    (a) Speedy demobilisation according to age and service
        group

    (b) Disciplinary action against the Commanding Officer of
        'Talwar' for alleged improper treatment of ratings

    (c) Best class of Indian food

    (d) R.N. scales of pay and family allowances

    (e) Retention of kit on release

    (f) Higher gratuity and Treasury pay on release, all
        demands to be decided in conjunction with a national
        leader whose name would be announced

████RD TELEGRAM

February and are still refusing duty.   20th February.
Situation in Bombay still very serious.   Majority of R.I.N.
ratings in Bombay numbering about 7,000 have joined in the
mutiny.   An incident during the night of 19/20th occurred
when approximately 120 ratings led by an Indian officer
attempted to force an entrance into the R.I.N. Central
Communication Office.   A number of windows were broken.
This party has now been arrested by Royal Marines.
Measures are in hand to control the mutineers and troops and
police have been detailed to assist in this should need
arise.   Civil, Naval and Military authorities in Bombay are
working in closest co-operation.   Admiral Godfrey, F.O.C.R.I.N.,
flew to Bombay this morning and will be joined there shortly by
General Lockhart, G.O.C. in C., Southern Command.

MESSAGE. IN

UNCLASSIFIED.   230755EF/February.

From.   F.O.C.R.I.N.   Date. 23.2.46.

                                Recd. 0920.

_____ P/L. _____

To.   R.I.N. General' Message 479IG.
IMMEDIATE.
        R.I.N. mutiny at Bombay has ended.

                                230755EF.

1st Lord.
1st S.L.(3)
2nd S.L.
V.C.N.S.
Secretary.
Parl. Secretary.
A.C.N.S.(O)
O.D.(2)
D.C.(2)
D. of P.(3)
M.(4)
R.I.N.L.O. London.

vms 109

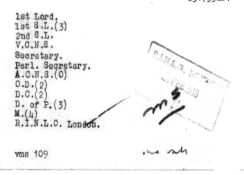

FELLOW COMMUNACATORS,

As YOU KNOW THAT COMMUNACATORS HAD ALWAYS BEEN AT THE FOREFRONT TO LEAD NATIONS, COUNTRIES ? DEFENCE FORCES ETC, INFORMATION OF ALL KINDS OF REFORMS,REVOLTS MUTINEES WERE SPREAD OUT BY COMMUNACATORS THROUGH OUT THE WORLD. THE LATEST MUTINEE OF 1946 IN THE RIN AND THE STRUGGLE TO PUT DOWN NHQ DECISIONS TO ABOLISH THE TOPPAS BRANCH FROM INDIAN NAVY ARE GLORIOUS EXAMPLES THE MOST EVENTS ARE ENLIGHTENED BY MR. B.C.DUTT IN THE MUTINEE OF OF INNOCENTS. MAIN CAUSES EXPLAINED BY HIM ARE :

1 FEUDAL PRACTICE BY OFFICERS.

2 BAD FOOD FOR RATINGS.

DO THESE PRACTICES NOT EXIST TODAY ? THEY DO !
EVEN MORE ARE ADDEDED BY OUR PRESENT OFFICERS : i.e.

1. SMUGGLING OF DUTY FREE VALUABLE GOVERNMENT ITEMS,

2. Rash mal and dirty behaviour of officers.

3. TAKING PERSONNEL WORK FROM US AND MANY MORE OTHER MISCHIEVOUS DOINGS,AS ALL OF US KNOW. BUT HOW CAN WE BE FREE FROM ALL THESE,IS THE QUESTTION TO BE SOLVED.

FREEDOM ALWAYS COMES THROUGH STRUGGLES,WHICH WE HAVE TO START.
LET ANY WORST CIRCUMSTANCES EXIST OR ARISE,BUT WE HAVE TO
CRUSH THEM BY TAKING SOME VERY CONCRETE   AND APPROPRIATE
ACTIONS BY UNITING OURSELVES INTO ONE BODY. AFTER ALL TO BUILD UP
A CONSCIOUS DISCIPLINE AMONG US.
MIND IT, WE SHALL RELY ON THE FORCES WE OURSELVES CREATE AND
ORGANIZE TO DEFEAT ALL THE REACTIONARY FORCES TO FIGHT FOR
HUMANLY DESERVED RIGHT,HOWEVER HARD AND TOUGH THE FIGHT MAY BE
NOTHING SHALL STOP US.
" CHANGE THE TREND OF INDIAN NAVY "
" UNITE AND ARISE TO ERADICATE THE WRONG DOINGS."

                                    YOURS,
                                    YOU ONLY.

Sources

1. 1946 Enquiry Commission report, set up by Government of India , headed by Chief Justice Sir Sayyid Fazal Ali with two judicial and two service members,-- 'Historical Back ground of RIN, Various mutinies in the Navy, and detailed description of causes & events of 1946 Naval Mutiny in various Naval stations.

2. Logs of Signal & Wireless communication between Navy/Military and various civil administrative authorities in India & abroad--- Reports & Administrative action/counter measures to control Naval Mutiny.

3. 'Reuters' Press releases, Bureau of Public Information reports' & Press communiqués issued during & after mutiny.

4. The suppressed version of Sailors Mutiny by Captain Scott who officiated as Senior Naval Officer Afloat in Bombay during mutiny--- Correspondence between RIN Liaison Officer & Admiralty/ Military Intelligence in UK

5. A passing reference to 'Occasional Paper No 11 of Centre of Armed Forces Historical Research' by Cmde King, Ex Commanding Officer HMIS *Talwar* during Naval Mutiny.